Encounter

Encounter

Experience God's Outrageous Love

Leanne O'Donnell

Copyright © 2021 by Leanne O'Donnell

Bible references, unless otherwise noted,
are quoted from the New Living Translation.

All rights reserved. No part of this publication may be reproduced, distributed, or transmitted in any form or by any means, including photocopying, recording, or other electronic or mechanical methods, without the prior written permission of the publisher, except in the case of brief quotations embodied in critical reviews and certain other noncommercial uses permitted by copyright law.

Paperback ISBN: 978-1-63337-550-5
E-book ISBN: 978-1-63337-551-2

Manufactured and printed in the United States of America

To my husband, Mike. This idea first came about because of you. I have experienced God so powerfully because of the adventurous journey that we've shared. We only found victory because we did it together. May you know how much I love you and that it pales in comparison to how mightily our God loves you.

To my kids—Hudson, Kellen, Macie, Graham, Grady, and Edison. My desire is that you experience God in life-changing ways and that you know yourselves as He sees you and I see you. You are wonderful people and you're dearly loved.

Part I
The Story

Why Love Matters

"LOVE ISN'T SOMETHING WE INVENTED. It's observable, powerful. It has to mean something... Maybe it's some evidence, an artifact of a higher dimension that we can't consciously perceive. I'm drawn across the universe to someone I haven't seen in a decade, who I know is probably dead. Love is the one thing we're capable of perceiving that transcends dimensions of time and space. Maybe we should trust that."

In the movie *Interstellar*, directed by Christopher Nolan, four scientists leave Earth to find a new planet in order to save the human race.[1] These brilliant academic minds who can explain almost everything in the universe with math come up against the unexplainable power and "otherness" of love. In one scene, the scientists are trying to decide which planet to visit based on the data they've gathered. Anne Hathaway's character wants to go to the planet where the man she loves has been stuck, awaiting rescue for ten years, but the data shows another planet may be a better option for survival. The quote above is her argument that her love could be guiding her, so she should pay attention to it.

The scientist describes love as a higher power, a force that transcends all other forces. She agrees that it doesn't make sense, but she argues that we can't ignore the sheer power of it just because we don't understand it. She is feeling something greater than herself that she can't quantify.

It's likely that she's sensing God, but she doesn't know it. The Bible tells us that God is love (1 Jn. 4:8). We don't often consider love to be the kind of powerful force that the character is describing. This gives us a different understanding of love and its role in my life. It's powerful! It transcends all barriers of life: culture, academia, language, everything. It's the one thing that transcends all things. And it's not a thing, but a Person. We need this Person of force, power, and transcendence in our lives.

If God is love, then nothing that God does is done outside of love. His actions are always loving. God's love fills the story of the earth all the way back to the beginning when God created the earth. Usually, we consider the creation account as a way to explain the origins of the earth. It tells us how we got here and what our purpose is on earth. But this isn't all that it shows us. The creation account of the Bible repeatedly shows us that God is a loving Creator.

Genesis 1 describes the Spirit of God as "hovering" over the waters. Some translations say "brooding." It's the same Hebrew word that's used to describe a mother hen incubating her chicks while waiting for them to hatch.[2] God was incubating the formless void waiting to bring forth new life. This image shows the care and focused attention of a loving parent. Brooding requires all of a mother's person—body, mind, and spirit—to be involved. The triune God was focused on nurturing life as He hovered over the waters.

Consider God breathing life into the dirt as He created Adam. He used His own breath to give life to a being that He was creating in His own image. God merely spoke the rest of creation into being, but man was different. God made Adam's creation intimate and personal using His very own breath.

God walked with Adam and Eve in the garden. When God made them, He cared about their well-being and valued their company. He said, "It's not good for man to be alone" (Gn. 2:18). "Man" here referring to humankind. God made Adam and Eve for each other because He knew they'd be better together. They were friends and partners in fulfilling the commission God gave them to take dominion over the earth.

God let Adam name the animals. He included Adam and Eve in the creation work. *No other thing that was created got to participate with God in creation the way Adam and Eve did.* God enjoyed their company and He wanted to partner with them. He wanted humans to partner with Him for their sake and for His sake. He *still wants* this relationship and partnership with us today.

After Adam and Eve ate the fruit, they hid from God. He gently questioned them about what happened. Then He made clothes for them. This act speaks volumes of God's heart for humanity. He didn't say, "You made your bed and now you'll have to lie in it!" He sought to help them and equip them for the life that was before them. He let them cover their shame. He even made the garments to cover them well. These animal skins were much better than any coverings they could've crafted for themselves. God doesn't make us expose ourselves and the shame that we carry. Sometimes He covers it for us until it's time to heal it.

All of these events show God's care and desire for humanity. The creation story shows us God's great love for His creation and for the people He created. David Benner more eloquently describes it this way:

Encounter

"Creation declares that humans are born of love and for love, created in the image of a God who is love. Love is our source and love is to be our fulfillment."[3]

Most people have heard that God loves them or that Jesus loves them. It's said so often that it might feel cliché. We all know the song that goes, "Jesus loves me this I know / For the Bible tells me so."

But what is love? What does it mean that God is love? What does it mean in our relationship with God? What are the implications of that in our lives? Does anything change because of God's love? Should it?

Because of these questions and deep need in my own life, I embarked on a journey to find myself and to find God. Many years ago when my life got especially difficult, I realized that the faith I had ascribed to for decades wasn't enough to get me through the difficulties I was facing. Either I needed to discover that there was more to who God was, or I needed to leave my faith on the curb. After a brief, failed attempt to forget God, I learned that I wasn't able to pretend He wasn't there, so I went looking for more with Him.

In the summer of 2013, I was beginning to feel a crisis rise up within my soul. I could see that I was not the woman, mom, or wife that I wanted to be. I felt contradiction and hypocrisy within me, but I didn't know what to do about it. Shortly before having my sixth baby, I had a mental breakdown. If there is ever a good time for a mental breakdown, this definitely wasn't it. I began to doubt everything about myself and my abilities. I cried for days and didn't know what was wrong. I just felt that I couldn't keep homeschooling my kids, I couldn't have another baby (although he was just three weeks away!), and I couldn't keep pretending I was okay. Except that I didn't know what was wrong.

I needed help. I called my mother-in-law on a Friday and explained my situation as best I could. I felt like a crazy person, but I didn't know what else to do. Without hesitation, she said that she would be at our house on Monday. She lived in Ohio and we lived in Colorado at the time, so this was no small feat.

She swept in like an angel and stayed with us for two weeks. She took care of the house and the kids. She put meals in the freezer and fed us every day. Most importantly, she spoke truth and encouragement to me. She helped me to re-orient so I could have my baby and care for my family (six kids, age ten and under). This wonderful blessing resulted in a great labor and delivery and a few weeks of peace. This act was one of the first times I experienced God's love intervening for me in such a powerful way.

I wish I could say that this was the end of it, but that was just the beginning of my challenging journey. After the baby was born, I experienced postpartum depression for the first time in my six pregnancies. I felt like I was sinking. The days were long and full. Our kids and home life relied on me and my ability to keep going, which may be the only reason I did keep going. I had a dear friend down the street who would check on me regularly and have my older kids to her house to play. She was a gift from God in that time of need.

Then, when our beloved sixth child was just six months old, my husband had a panic attack that triggered an avalanche of debilitating fear, anxiety, and panic that ended up lasting for five years. Of course, throughout the journey we didn't know how long it would last. Many days it felt like it would last forever. Most of the time, it felt like we couldn't endure it one more day.

These experiences provoked a season of soul-searching and God-searching. I thought I knew God well. I had been walking with Him and seeking Him for about fifteen years at that time. I knew the Bible well. I had heard God speak and had seen Him provide for my family and me in amazing ways, but that foundation wasn't enough to carry me through this dark season. I needed more. I needed to know myself better and discover God in new ways.

At the church we attended, one of the pastors started talking about soul care. It was something I'd never heard of before, and I obviously needed something different, so this seemed like a good place to begin digging. Soul care is the practice of maintaining a healthy soul. Soul being defined as a person's mind, will, and emotions. Soul care usually involves spiritual formation practices, counseling, quiet time, exercise, spiritual direction, and healthy community. Soul care also involves inner healing of childhood wounds, and identifying and replacing lies one believes about himself and about God.

I started focusing on soul care by reading books about the contemplative life, exploring imaginative prayer, and seeing a spiritual director. I learned to sit with God in silence and stillness. I learned to hear God through Scripture by considering small passages and asking Him questions about them. I learned to pay attention to my inner world.

As a next step, I decided to pursue spiritual direction training for myself. Spiritual direction is a practice of accompanying another in their faith journey. The director is trained to ask questions to help the directee see and hear God in ways that he or she didn't notice before. I wish I could say that I wanted to pursue spiritual direction to help other people, but at the time that wasn't true. I wanted something to help me. I also wanted to pursue something for myself beyond the mundanity of everyday life. I'm thankful that God will use whatever motive we have to offer.

My husband and I spent a year in Colorado fighting to make ends meet while fighting our internal battles. That sounds like a bad joke. And many days it felt like one to both of us. After a year, we realized that we couldn't do it by ourselves. God wasn't providing for us to stay there, but He opened provision for us to move back to Ohio. So, we packed up our six kids and moved back to Ohio to live in my in-laws' house. They lovingly offered us a place of refuge so we could get through this season and hopefully overcome this crisis we faced. They provided a good example of the significance of community support in soul care.

During that time in their house, we did everything we could to get well. We saw counselors, read books, listened to sermons, studied nutrition, visited nutritionists, studied multiple kinds of inner healing, and practiced the many techniques we learned. We surrendered, we trusted God, we fought, and we doubted, over and over again.

The most difficult thing about a season like this is the inability to explain what's happening. You don't really understand why you feel the way you do. St. John of the Cross coined this experience a "dark night of the soul." In the book *The Critical Journey* by Janet Hagberg and Robert A. Guelich, this season is described as "hitting The Wall." In secular counseling, it's called a midlife crisis. Regardless of what you call it, if someone hasn't experienced it, then they don't really understand. In fact, we didn't really understand. We just knew that so much was wrong, and we couldn't figure out how to make it right. We needed God to make it right.

During my spiritual direction training, I read a book by David Benner called *Surrender to Love*. This book changed my understanding of the love God offers His children. While reading it, I learned that God's love is much greater than I'd ever understood. In fact, God's love wasn't something I'd ever spent much time thinking about. Benner explained the depth and power of God's love as well as the importance of choosing to live in it. With this new understanding, I didn't have to base my faith only on what I read in the Bible or other people's experiences. I could have my own experiences of God to strengthen and renew me every day. Learning to experience God for myself changed everything!

Theologian A.W. Tozer says that we can know God's love "as certainly as we know material things through our five senses."[4] I would like to invite you into the possibility that you too can experience God's love for yourself.

Did you know it was possible to experience God's love? Depending on your upbringing and church experience, this could be your normal understanding of God, or it could sound close to heresy. Regardless of where you are, there is always more with God. He wants to lead you into more of who you are and more of what He has for you in a deeper relationship with Himself.

Pause for a moment and consider the following question. You may know in your mind, and even in your heart, that God loves you. But have you ever had an experience where you could *feel* God's love for you?

Your Roots

IN HIS FAMOUS LETTER to the Ephesians, the Apostle Paul uses powerful imagery to convey the truth of God's love toward us. He writes:

> Then Christ will make his home in your hearts as you trust in him. Your roots will grow down into God's love and keep you strong. And may you have the power to understand, as all God's people should, how wide, how long, how high, and how deep his love is. May you *experience* the love of Christ, though it is too great to understand fully. Then you will be made complete with all the fullness of life and power that comes from God (Eph. 3:17–19 NLT, emphasis mine).

This verse is the heart of this book. It says that God's love keeps us strong, but only if we know it, believe it, and claim it. We must experience it.

Encounter

Consider this imagery. Imagine the roots of a mighty oak, reaching deep into the soil to be nourished so that the tree may grow ever higher into the expanse of heaven. This allows the tree to become more of what it's made to be in strength and health. The roots must run deep in order for the tree to stand tall and strong. With strong roots, a tree has great potential to thrive for centuries as one of the tallest of God's creations. Without strong roots, the tree will easily fall over in a substantial wind. You are like that tree. If you have strong roots in God's love, there are no limits to what you can do in Christ. But you can only reach your potential if your roots run deep.

The writers of Scripture use the imagery of a tree in other places to help us better understand this great mystery. For us to flourish in the truth of God's love is to be like a tree planted by living waters, bearing fruit that lasts (Psalm 1). It is to be connected to the source of Life itself, a well that springs up and never runs dry (John 4). Jesus said that we have been chosen by God, because of His love, and appointed to bear fruit (John 15:9–17). God wants us to understand how significant it is for us to be rooted and nourished in His love. It is our very life force.

Looking back, I see that my faith felt insufficient because my roots weren't strong enough. As I began to experience God's love for me, my roots began to grow deeper, so I was able to grow. The transformation was slow. The enduring kind always is. At first, knowing God's love just helped me feel safe in tumultuous circumstances.

We were living in my in-laws house and my husband had slipped into a more severe stage of anxiety. He had tried working, but it was becoming too difficult even for him to leave the house. Experiencing God's love was assuring me that it wasn't our fault and that God was allowing this to fix beliefs and heal wounds in each of us that had been broken for a long time. His love showed me that He was taking care of me. This began to fill a deep void of insecurity within me.

YOUR ROOTS

As I went about surviving each day, I began to see God's love for me in ways I hadn't noticed before. I was connected with a wonderful pastoral counselor who supported and encouraged me in ways that allowed me to feel safe enough to let my guard down. This was new for me. I'd spent my life up to that point living under layers of self-protection. In this safe relationship, I was able to be honest and discover what was going on in my heart. It was clear that this soon-to-be friend was showing me the Father's heart for me.

At one point, my husband and I decided that I would get a full-time job so my husband could stay home with the kids and heal. God provided a great job for me as an event coordinator at a downtown venue. I had zero experience and was nervous, but God assured me that He was with me and would equip me to do it.

I saw His love for me in the provision and favor I received. I saw His love in my ability to learn something new and excel at it. I loved this job! I loved working with couples and creating amazing wedding days for them. It turned out I was good at it. There were many times that I was able to encourage a bride or even share wisdom for a problem she was facing. I felt God's deep love for me in discovering gifts that I didn't know I had and being able to work a job I really enjoyed that I never would've tried otherwise.

I was beginning to see in a new way what Paul meant when he said God's love has height, depth, breadth, and width. Because even while God was healing my husband and healing me, He was also showing me who I was and giving me loving gifts. He's always doing multiple things through every situation.

In this idea of height, depth, breadth, and width, Paul is saying that God's love is a multi-dimensional love. Have you ever noticed that Paul is referring to four dimensions of space, but we only live in three? Before

Encounter

experiencing God, this wording just seemed like a nice analogy, but now I see it differently.

If you've ever watched superhero or sci-fi movies, you've heard reference to multiple dimensions beyond the ones in which we live on earth. *Interstellar* is a perfect example. When the characters are on one planet for ten minutes, they've lost *years* on earth. In the Marvel movie *Antman*, the characters explore the quantum realm where time and space are considered to be irrelevant. I say all this to point out that humanity is aware of something greater, something beyond ourselves. Even those who deny the existence of God are aware of the greatness of the universe and that there are complexities that we have only barely tapped into. I began to understand this awareness of multiple dimensions as indicators of the dimensions of God and His heart.

God is showing us just how vast He is. He's given us imagination and knowledge to show us that we can't know everything about our universe. No matter what we discover, there is so much more that we don't know or understand. This is who God is. This vastness of His person also expresses the great love that He has for His people and His creation. His love expands farther than the universe, reaches to every dimension imaginable, is nearer than your skin, more complex than quantum physics, and yet as simple as a smile. God's love is everything we need it to be and more. We just need to *know* it.

We must also believe it. We must believe that it's real for us and ask to see it. We must reach out in faith expecting to see God answer our call. It takes some time and intention on our part as well, but the investment is worth it. It only gets richer the deeper you're willing to go with God. And He will take you as far as you're willing to go with Him. There's always more of Him to see, experience, and know. This is what God wants for all of us.

YOUR ROOTS

In this season of healing and full-time work, one of the things that God pressed upon my heart was that there is always more of Him and what He has to give me. I knew this because He spoke it to me in a quiet time with Him and it anchored deep in my heart. I chose to believe that God really had *more* for me, and it turned out that He did. God used my job as an event coordinator to change me and grow me in many ways. He was molding me to be more of the person He made me to be.

I experienced God through a mentor He gave me at work. This manager showed me God's heart for me through his encouragement, support, and teaching. He never condemned me, but always showed trust and compassion. It was abundantly clear that this was another way that God was caring for me and showing me His love. He used a servant who had no idea of his impact.

Another gift God gave was expanding my capacity for life. My job required that I manage and organize various people and events daily. I was planning thirty to forty weddings at all times. Imagine all those brides, their moms, decorations, and details! I was also being a wife and mom of six at home. Through that job, I gained greater mental and emotional capacities to handle life and stressful situations. I learned that I'm a planner and have the gift of administration. It was just two years that I worked this job, but I planned and executed over eighty weddings.

This new awareness of myself gave me confidence in who I was and what I was capable of. This was a mighty gift from God in a time when I was just trying to survive. God in his goodness and love gifted me with so much more than I expected through my experience of Him. My roots were growing deeper in His love.

To Know and Be Known

I HOPE MY STORY AND PAUL'S WORDS in Ephesians 3 make it clear that it is *essential* for us to experience God's love. Experiencing His love, more than just knowing about it, is how we become who we are made to be. When the Bible speaks of knowing God, it's a different meaning than our English word that means "to know." In English, we most often use "knowing" to mean being aware of something or someone. We *know* they exist. But in Hebrew, "to know" means to have a personal, intimate relationship with that person.[5] It's an experiential knowing. In order to know God, we must experience Him. In the same way that you can't really know another person without interacting with them, knowing and experiencing God are inseparable.

The Merriam-Webster website defines the word "experience" as "the fact or state of having been affected by or gained knowledge through *direct observation or participation*." It's the difference between hearing information from someone else versus knowing something because you've seen it or done it yourself. I can tell you that God loves you, but it will never hold the same power as hearing it directly from Him.

Think of all the things we know in our heads but have no life experience to support. People regularly say they like famous actors or athletes who they don't actually know. They know about that person, their public persona, and have seen them in movies or sports, but they don't have an experience of them.

Similarly, I have always wanted to visit France. I studied French for seven years in high school and college. I like museums and history, so I want to see the Louvre, the Eiffel Tower, and Pont Neuf. I am enchanted by the romance of Paris, the French Riviera, and the South of France. I want to go there, and I'm pretty sure I would love it. But the truth remains: I've never been there. I only know about it, and many of my ideas and expectations could be misinformed.

In contrast, I *know* that I love Colorado, because I have experienced Colorado. I lived there for six years, and there was little that I didn't like about it. I experienced Colorado in so many different ways. I saw the majesty of the Rocky Mountains, enjoyed the clean, crisp air at high elevation, the constant sunshine, and the bluest sky I've ever seen. My six years living in Colorado were like the first deep breath of my life. I loved it, and I always will.

In the same way, when you experience God, you know Him personally, and no one can take that away from you. You will know that you know that you know that God is real and that God is with you and for you.

You've probably heard many stories of children who "wouldn't take their parents' word for it," but had to experience something for themselves and "learn the hard way." Although it's unhealthy to live motivated by rebellion, this desire to explore and experience life is good. In much the same spirit, God expects us to know Him by experiencing Him for ourselves within the boundaries He has set for us. We are designed to participate in our lives, try new things, and learn from our experiences, both good and bad. If you've ever watched a toddler play, you know what I mean.

God made us to learn, explore, and question. He made us to engage in our lives and to engage Him so that we can fully enjoy life and all He created for us. He wanted us to have the courage and curiosity to create and discover. He gave us a mighty purpose when he told Adam, "Be fruitful and increase in number; fill the earth and subdue it. Rule over the fish in the sea and the birds in the sky and over every living creature that moves on the ground" (Gen. 1:28). Man and Woman were the pinnacle of God's creation. They were made in His image and were supposed to work with Him to create a beautiful world, and He equipped them accordingly. He gave us curiosity, imagination, and an adventurous spirit so we would find Him and do what we're made to do.

He was among humanity in the garden so He could work hand in hand with His people. His desire was for regular fellowship with them. I imagine Adam and Eve sharing with Him what they were learning and experiencing. They likely discussed problem-solving ideas, exploration of the garden, and joy over what they learned and saw.

Obviously, this was much different before the fall, when Adam and Eve still walked unhindered with God in the garden. Although things changed after the fall, the plan didn't change. God still desires to partner with His people and walk in fellowship with them. We see this kind of fellowship in the lives of Abraham, Moses, and David and the ways they walked with God. We are invited to walk with God in the same way today.

When Jesus came, He set things right between humanity and God. No more sin offerings, no more animal sacrifices. No more fear of being destroyed by a holy God. Jesus paid the price for all sin, punishment, judgment, and shortcomings. He made us blameless and righteous by His death and resurrection. This is the power of God's love. He made a way for humanity to easily come to Him and He wants us to experience this outrageous love in every area of our lives.

It's not just limited to salvation and going to heaven someday. There are so many other good things that God gives us through Jesus's resurrection—healing, prosperity, joy, peace, and freedom from fear and lies—just to name a few. When you take the first steps to experience God through these exercises, you're choosing to believe that He is as good and loving as the Bible says He is and that He wants to give you all of these good things.

Once you have experienced God's love for you, you know beyond a shadow of a doubt that you can trust Him. Being confident of God's great love for you allows you to give your cares and worries to Him. Otherwise, it's easy to doubt if He actually cares about your situation. When you've experienced His love, then you will be able to move into a life of action fueled by faith. If you're grounded in God's love, you won't despair while waiting for Him to answer your prayers because you're confident He's faithful and trustworthy. When you know His love, you will have the courage to live life boldly.

Experiencing God's love becomes the crucial foundation on which the rest of your faith journey is built. It empowers you to become the person God made you to be, the person you dream of becoming.

Barriers

EXPERIENCING GOD can allow you to see Him with fresh eyes and see your whole life through a different lens of grace, goodness, and love, but there are many reasons that experiencing God can be difficult. We have no framework for interaction with a spiritual being who we can't see. It's also difficult to imagine that this Being we can't see could love us as much as I'm telling you. Paul says in Eph. 3:19 that God's love is "too great to fully understand." Well, of course! We have so many limitations in our humanity. We are physical matter and God is spirit. We are bound by time and space. He is not. We don't know what we don't know. We also live under a curse, bound by sin.

I don't want to discourage you. I want to cut off any arguments that may come up before you even begin this journey. It's difficult to grasp in your intellectual mind how to experience God until you have done it. But when you step out in faith, believing that He has more for you, He will, indeed, show up for you in ways you didn't know were possible. This is part of the mystery that Paul tells us about throughout his letters—we can interact with a God we can't see who loves us and wants to give us good things.

Let's talk about some of the barriers and squash them. You have an enemy who is actively working to keep you from knowing God and His love. He will keep pushing doubts, fear, and lies to keep you from hoping for more with God. Paul wrote to remind us that *nothing can separate* us from the love of God in Christ Jesus (Rom.8:38-39). The enemy can't separate you from God, but he can try to keep you from *believing* God's love for you is true or trying to experience Him more. I don't like to give the enemy too much credit, but we can't forget that he's real or we won't be aware of his tactics. His tactics are lies and fear. That's it. If we're aware of lies and fear, and seek God to remove them, we'll go a long way.

Another barrier to experiencing God is the busyness of life. We're all running on the hamster wheel of achievement and hurry. Unfortunately, we get so focused on what we think life should be that we forget to include the Author of life in it. I am guilty of that. Regularly, I must remind myself to slow down and fix my eyes on Jesus. It's a mindset of being aware of God and turning your attention toward him regularly throughout your days. It only takes a few seconds, but it can open your awareness to God's active presence in your life.

It's important to be intentional to make time to be with God. It can feel like a burden, but when I think of all the silly things I make time for in my day, I realize that there is enough time for this. And don't I *want* time to be with God? Yes! How easily I get distracted and forget. It's all about how we choose to use our time.

We all have broken histories that have shaped our beliefs. We've all been hurt by other people in our lives. Oftentimes these beliefs shape our image of God and keep us from trusting Him. Many times these experiences lead us to believe lies about God and ourselves. When you begin to experience God's love, you are finally able to have a strong enough foundation to see the lies you believe and have the courage to let Jesus heal them. Then you can forgive those who hurt you. This, in turn, allows you to see God for who He really is.

As I experienced God, I found a lot of inner healing. God showed me parts of my past that He wanted to heal. It was never about blaming others, but about acknowledging my heart and the hurts that caused me to believe lies about myself. One of the most significant lies I believed throughout my life was that I was alone. Many of my memories of growing up are of being alone—alone at home after school, alone on bike rides, alone during the summer, alone in the hallways at school, alone in my bedroom. God showed me that it was a lie I believed. My belief skewered my perspective and caused me to forget all the good times I had with my family and friends, all the times I wasn't alone. I only saw through the lens of the lie. When I talked to Him about it, Jesus would show up in my memories.

In one memory of being alone, Jesus showed me that He was with me before I even knew Him. In another memory of myself as a baby, God gave me a vision of angels circling my bed. He was showing me that He was with me and protecting me. He showed me that I was never alone, and I never had to fend for myself or figure life out by myself. This opened my eyes to see that what I remembered may not have been reality. That belief had negatively affected my friendships, my marriage, and my kids. During this profound season, God called out those lies that I didn't know I had and began to heal them with His love and truth. Now I no longer feel alone!

The good news is that you aren't stuck in these lies. God wants to make you aware of the areas of brokenness that have been dictating your

Encounter

life and heal them in you. This is when you're truly free to live out of your heart and be the person you're made to be!

Another barrier comes from our view of love. The relationships that shape us also shape our understanding of love. The love we know from family, friends, caretakers, leaders, spouses, and others is flawed even in the healthiest relationships. For those who've known abuse or neglect, the idea of a loving God may not even compute. The pain in life makes it easy to believe that all authority is broken, all love is selfish, and no one cares for you except you. The reality is that none of us have experienced human love that is not tarnished by selfishness, fear, or pain. Motives can be misguided or misunderstood. One person can give for his own sake. A child can misinterpret actions and intentions. We live in a fallen world, so relationships are hard. God wants us to experience His perfect love, so that we can freely give and receive love in relationships.

We keep talking about this perfect love from a perfect Father who wants good for us. If you've never known this kind of love on earth, how can you experience it from God? It's another barrier. Imagine a child who has never seen a picture of an elephant or been to a zoo. If you are trying to describe an elephant to this child, you would need to reference animals that she does know. You might say, "It's like a horse, but bigger. It has a long nose that looks like a snake that makes a trumpet sound. It's gray and has big feet." She will see in part, but she won't really get it unless she gets to see an elephant. The same is true for us as we seek to know the love of God that is "too great to fully understand." We won't be able to see differently until we experience love from Him. To do this we must confront our brokenness and consider that our images of God might be inaccurate. Seeing perfect love will require giving Him the opportunity to show you what is true about who He is. It will require great faith.

BARRIERS

There are lots of things that get in the way of us being able to experience God, but Paul doesn't sit on these realities. Because Paul is praying for us to "experience the love of Christ," we know that it is possible. These barriers that we have discussed are no challenge to God. He will gladly free us from them so we can know Him. Paul says that God longs for us to know what we *are able* to understand. I invite you to delight in the possibility of what God wants to show you. I want to encourage you that there is more to God than you've experienced so far. Believe that He can heal the brokenness in your heart. Trust that God is different than any negative perceptions you carry. When you begin to experience God and know Him, everything changes.

My heart for this book is that you will encounter God in powerful ways and that your heart and life will be transformed as your roots grow deep into His love.

God's Promises

WHEN MY LIFE STARTED FALLING APART back in 2013, it was God's promises that helped me endure. I had done a lot of Bible study and knew that God promised to take care of his people. Even though I hadn't experienced Him very deeply, I trusted that He would do what He'd promised, so we would be okay. As I continued to seek Him and began to have experiences of hearing from Him, the promises I had to rest on increased. When He told me that I wasn't alone, I trusted that. When He told me that He had more for us, I believed Him. At one point, He assured me that He was carrying me in His arms every day, and that gave me grace to endure. God's promises to us are the starting point for our ability to experience Him.

    The spiritual exercises in this book each start with a promise from the Bible. Hebrews 4:12 says, "For the word of God is alive and powerful." That means it isn't static. It moves. More practically, a verse may mean something to you one day and then mean something completely

Encounter

different another day, depending on your circumstances and what God wants to show you. Expect that God will speak to you through His word. Expect to hear more than just what's written on the page.

Earlier I mentioned that God promised He had more for me. The day it happened I was reading in Joshua 2 about Rahab. I had read that story many times, but this day it was different. I asked God what He wanted to show me about Himself from this story. He said, "I'm a God of more." When God speaks to you, you know it because it resonates within your spirit. He had so much more for Rahab than she could have imagined. He was telling me that He also had so much more for me. I understood that no matter where I was or what I did, learned, or experienced, He would always have more to offer me in my journey with Him. He is limitless and He will go as far and deep as I am willing to go with Him. This is the difference between just reading the Bible and reading it with the expectation that God will meet you through it.

Because I was seeing life through this lens of His love and experiencing Him, I was devouring the Bible to know Him more. I suddenly saw the Old Testament with greater depth and heart than I had before. The Old Testament became a picture of who God is. But I didn't see an angry, war-mongering God. I saw a loving, gentle Father who was seeking to draw His people to Himself and show them the very things He was showing me. It's the same message He's had for all people throughout the history of the world. It's always been about God's love and desire for relationship with humanity. So much so that He sent His Son to die for our sins so that nothing could keep us apart from Him.

Many of the passages that we will use to encounter God are from the Old Testament. It is rich with imagery that captures God's heart for His people. Some people question how the Old Testament applies to us because it was written for the Israelites before the redemptive work of

Christ. While it was written *to* the Nation of Israel and is about them, it is also written *for* us. Paul makes it clear in Romans 11:17 that those who come to a saving faith in Jesus are grafted into God's family with Israel. We are now heirs of God's promises (Gal. 3:29), so these promises are for us too! We can also draw from the stories of the Old Testament encounters between God and His people to learn about Him. They teach us His character and His heart. They show us how much God desires to know His people and be known by them. He is still the same God who breathed life into Adam, spoke to David, and appeared to Paul.

The stories of the Old Testament contribute to its significance. The New Testament is largely instruction. Instruction is good and necessary, but stories speak to our hearts. Stories have the ability to transcend time, culture, and space to share a message. This is why people study literature. The stories of the Old Testament give us a rich picture of God. For example, we learn through Abraham how God cares for us when we make mistakes. We learn in Joshua how powerful God is against our enemies. We see through Daniel God's response to a faithful decision to choose Him above all else. Through the Babylonian exile, we see how God equips His people for prosperity in trying situations (Jer. 29:7). He shows us through Nehemiah that He responds to the faith of just one person who will stand firm. This is His heart toward us and because of the finished work of Christ, we are always covered in His grace, favor, and righteousness. We never have to offer sacrifices to be right with Him. We can walk boldly into His presence trusting that He adores us and wants to give us good things.

Many of the scripture passages I use are from the Psalms. David is called a man after God's own heart (1 Sam. 13:14), so it makes sense that David's psalms lead us to a greater understanding of God's heart for us. David's psalms are unique because they are refreshingly honest. David speaks of overwhelming emotions like depression, anger, and fear. He declares his desire for God to destroy His enemies and smash their teeth (Ps. 3:7). I know Jesus told us to bless our enemies, but it's important to first be honest with God about how we're feeling. David gives us a great example of how brutally honest we can be with God.

Even though David speaks of great despair, he always remembers the goodness of God and ends his psalms by praising God. David didn't ignore his emotions, but he never got stuck in them either. This pattern of honestly expressing one's self then moving into trust and praise is a good template for us to follow in our healing journey. Then we can move toward healing, forgiveness, and freedom.

Experiencing God

GOD IS ALWAYS PRESENT WITH US. He is also always positioned toward us. That never changes. Unfortunately, we are often distracted by the busyness of life, too focused on our fears, or simply not paying attention, so we don't notice that God is moving around us.

I've heard many people say that they've looked for God and not found Him. They blame God because He didn't show up when they asked or in the ways they expected to see Him. Oftentimes God chooses to reveal Himself in unexpected ways. He is not a predictable God and He doesn't appear on command.

For centuries, the Jews were anticipating a Messiah who would conquer their enemies and set up a kingdom on earth. In fact, God promised them He would give them a kingdom and a Messiah who was King. The problem was that there was a large part of the plan that God didn't tell them. He wasn't setting up His kingdom when He came the first time.

Instead, Jesus defeated death by way of the cross with plans to come a second time. Because Jesus didn't come the way they expected, so they missed the Messiah they had been longing for.

You might be waiting for a particular answer, and His provision for you is not what you want. When I prayed for healing for my husband and provision for my family, I didn't want to live in my in-law's house. I told God multiple times that I didn't like His provision. The truth was my pride was hurt. I was ashamed and embarrassed about how my situation appeared to others. If I had rejected God's provision, I would've missed so many good gifts from Him. He knew that what He planned to give me through this situation was greater than the discomfort I felt.

We need to look for Him where He is instead of where we expect Him to be. In the book *Silence* by Shūsaku Endō, the characters believe that God has abandoned them because He hasn't ended their suffering. He doesn't seem to be responding to their pleas. He is silent. But the priest says, "But our Lord was not silent. Even if he had been silent, my life until this day would have spoken of him." We just need to learn how to recognize Him.

Because God is alive, and because He is eager to be with you, you can expect to hear from Him as often as you seek Him. Be open to finding Him anywhere. He's in your workplace, your home, and nature. He's in your emotions, desires, mind, and imagination. He works through other people and the Bible to meet you and speak to you. The Bible is a gift to help us know this invisible Being and how to interact with Him. The people in the Bible show us that it's possible. It's encouraging us to do the same. He longs to share life with us.

Upon starting this journey, it's important to *desire* to hear from God. You must believe that He speaks and that He wants to speak to you. If you've never heard from God and you would like to, the best thing to do is to ask Him. Tell Him that you want to hear from Him.

EXPERIENCING GOD

As a young believer, I read *The Hiding Place* by Corrie ten Boom. In the book, Corrie writes of how she asked God to speak to her, and He did. I thought that if it worked for her, then maybe I could ask Him too and He would speak to me. Sure enough, not long after I prayed that prayer, I heard from God in new ways.

One thing I want to clarify is that when I say "God speaks" or "hearing from God," I'm referring to any of the ways God communicates. Typically, when God speaks it's not an audible voice, although it can be. Sometimes it's a phrase that comes to mind. Sometimes it's an awareness of something like a new thought or idea. Sometimes His answer is just a deep knowing within yourself. Some people see pictures, others journal and find God's words in what they've written. There are many ways. Don't limit yourself to what you expect or what you'd prefer. Instead, be open to consider that many things could be God speaking to you.

A common question I get from people is, "How do you know if the thoughts in your head are from you or from God?" There are many ways to know. It's important to remember that when you are saved, you are given the mind of Christ. This means you can think God's thoughts and He can use your thoughts, imagination, and dreams to speak to you. Notice the tone of what you hear. His voice just sounds different than my voice. God talks kindly to me and I don't usually talk kindly to myself. Do you often speak to yourself in life-giving ways? The voice of God is always gentle and life-giving, even in correction. I've been corrected by God and it was delivered with so much love that I didn't feel corrected. I felt excited to change that behavior or attitude he mentioned because I knew it would help me.

You can also test what you're hearing to see if it is consistent with Scripture. If it's God, it will always be supported by the Bible. Another way to know God is speaking is if other people tell you the same thing. If a person tells me the same thing I think God told me, then I take that as confirmation that I heard correctly. The more you practice hearing from Him, the more familiar you will become with His voice. "His sheep follow Him because they know His voice," Jesus says in John chapter 10. You will know when you hear from God because His voice will give you a peace and joy that can only come from Him.

You may wonder, "If His voice is the same as Scripture, why do we need to hear from Him? Why would He bother to speak to me now if He has already spoken through Scripture?" The Bible is only part of what God has given us. Don't misunderstand me. It's a very important part and I use it regularly to interact with God. It is there as a foundation for us know God and seek Him, but it's not all of what He wants to say.

He's also given us the Holy Spirit to teach us and remind us (John 14:26). Imagine a beloved family member or friend who you are very close to. If that person wrote you a letter describing their love for you, you would read it again and again, but that wouldn't be the end of your relationship. You would expect to spend time with them, talk to them, and hear their voice repeatedly. You would seek them out for the beauty and joy of their company. It's not possible to have a relationship if you don't spend time with that person and have continual interactions with them.

Here are a couple different examples of ways that God speaks. These are by no means the only ways, but these might help someone new to hearing from God. One common way that God speaks is through Scripture. This is more than just reading the words printed on the page as I mentioned before. There are times when the words of the Bible seem different when you read them with expectation. The Holy Spirit shows up, the Word becomes alive, and phrases begin to stand out like they're being highlighted just for you. Verses that you hadn't noticed before begin to emerge and you receive new insights from them. Those verses begin to mean something different to you in a way that is specific to your life circumstances at that moment.

The first time this happened to me I was reading Jeremiah 29. I was having trouble knowing what to read that day, so I went to a tried-and-true passage. I was a stay-at-home mom at the time with a two-year-old, a four-year-old, and a baby on the way. Mothering and staying home were what I wanted, but it was proving to be a difficult journey for me. Many days I felt like a fish out of water. I needed some encouragement, and I looked to this familiar passage for some light.

As I read verses 12–14, something powerful began to happen. It was as though God was in the room with me. The words seemed to jump off the page. It was like I was reading them in surround sound, and they filled my heart and mind with hope. I knew that God was promising me that He was hearing me and that He would answer me. He was promising that He would lead me out of "captivity and restore my fortunes." I wasn't a physical slave, but I was a slave in my mindsets. I needed to know that I wouldn't feel this way forever. This encounter with Him through the Word assured me that things would change. Ironically, the healing journey I share here is the answer to that promise He gave me eight years prior. God heard the cry of my heart, and He used the Bible and Holy Spirit to speak.

Another way to hear from God is through words or phrases that pop into your mind. These can seem like random or untethered thoughts, but they have a different flavor than your everyday thinking. One difference is that they aren't usually the kind of thoughts you think on your own. These thoughts are life-giving and full of grace, loving toward self, solution-oriented, and other-oriented. God can speak to you this way at any time. I've had these insights from Him come when I least expect them, when I'm not even thinking about Him. If you start to acknowledge these thoughts as God speaking and respond to them, God will speak to you even more because you're faithfully stewarding them.

The first time this happened to me I was not reading the Bible or having quiet time. I was standing in my kitchen, feeling helpless, crying out to God because of the ways I felt inadequate as a parent. I was certain that I was a terrible parent, and I felt like a constant failure to my children. I cried out loud to God, "Why do You let me do this?" Instantly, I heard a clear response flash through my mind. *It's so they know they need a Savior.* This stopped me in my tracks. I knew it was God because I would never think something like that myself. I knew because it filled me with peace in that moment of anguish. It didn't come in a spirit of judgement or condemnation like I would've heaped on myself. In hearing the phrase, I felt grace and compassion. Only God can do that! I was able to receive His grace in that moment in a way that I never could have without hearing from Him. His words are still with me today and have carried me through many stressful parenting moments.

A third way we can hear from God is through our sanctified imagination. This makes some people nervous and skeptical. For hundreds of years, creativity and imagination have been shunned as frivolous, inessential, and unreliable. Let me tell you why you can trust your imagination. When you are saved, you are given the mind of Christ (1 Cor. 2:16) and you have the Holy Spirit within you. Your imagination is a part of your mind. God created it and He sanctified it for His use. Another reason is that our God is a creative God. He made the whole universe out of an expression of His own imagination. Things that didn't exist before were called into being. To do that requires an incredible imagination! God has an imagination, and we are made in His image, so it stands to reason that He gave us an imagination like His, and He intended for us to use it.

It is not in using our imagination where the fault lies. Just like anything else in the world, it can be used incorrectly. If we use it as an escape, or to twist God's ways into our own wills, then we're misusing it. If we pretend that God is someone different than who He is revealed to be in the Bible, then we err with our imagination. There are so many good ways you can use your imagination. You can imagine Jesus with you throughout your day. He says that He is, so why wouldn't we consider it. One of my friends said she sees Him sitting in her passenger seat every time she's driving her car. This has helped her develop friendship and intimacy with Him.

You can also find God in artwork, nature, and music as you invite the Holy Spirit to speak through your imagination. Many times I've imagined that blowing tree branches are the trees waving their arms praising God. I've imagined a gentle breeze as God's tender touch and the warm sun on my face as His presence. At church, we experience God in music. The words create mental pictures that we enter to seek God. When we seek God and commit our minds to Him, our imagination is a wonderful tool to interact with Him.

God can also use your imagination to better understand Scripture. You can imagine a Bible story in order to fully grasp what was happening then and to apply it to yourself today. For example, if you can imagine God defending and protecting Israel at the Red Sea, then you can imagine Him defending and protecting you in powerful ways in your own life. I love to imagine myself by "still waters" with Jesus as I read Psalm 23. I can feel His rest and care for me, then I recall that imagery and feeling at times when I need peace.

A few years ago, I was reading Joshua 3. As I was reading it, my spirit began to stir within me. I could sense that God had something for me in that passage. I only read verses 1–5 because that seemed like a good place to stop. Then, I meditated on those five verses and reread them multiple times.

As I read, I imagined the priests giving the Israelites instructions. I pictured the whole scene in my head, even filling in details that weren't mentioned in the text. Then I dwelt on the verses that the Holy Spirit highlighted for me: "Since you have never traveled this way before, they will guide you. Stay about half a mile behind them, keeping a clear distance between you and the Ark. Make sure you don't come any closer." Because I could imagine it all in my mind, I could then begin talking to God about it for my own life and listening for His response.

"God," I prayed, "I'm journeying a way I have never been before. Thank You for meeting me here. You know how much I hate to get lost and how I struggle with security. What else, God?" I sat and waited. I could feel God's presence with me and His heart for me as I waited. I knew that because of Jesus I didn't have to keep a distance from God like the Israelites did. I knew the instructions were there to protect the Israelites, but what did they have to do with me? I sat quietly and thought through these things.

It was then that God gave me an image of a circle in the Israelite camp. I saw myself sitting right in the middle of it with the Ark on the edge of the circle in front of me. In that moment I knew what God was showing me. The circle was His will, and He was telling me that I would feel safe if I stayed in the center of it. He was cautioning me that to go too close to the edges of His will was trying to see too far ahead. I was walking too close to the edges every time I fought to control events in my life that were beyond my control. He was inviting me to surrender and trust Him.

He wanted me to feel safe and cared for and showed me that would happen if I simply sat in the middle of His will without trying to see ahead to the next steps. This vision made it clear in ways that words could not fully express. There's a knowing from the Holy Spirit that fills you in these moments. You just know that it's God, because only God can give you these kinds of life-giving insights.

Imagination can also help you fill in details of the Bible that aren't included in the text. If you're reading about Jesus walking down the street to see Zacchaeus, imagine the longing that caused Zacchaeus to climb the tree. Imagine how Zacchaeus felt when Jesus looked at him and said his name. Then, it's only a small step to imagine Jesus looking at you and saying your name. Imagination is necessary for this. We aren't changing the stories. Filling in missing details doesn't change the truth of what God is sharing, it enhances it.

During Advent last year, I attended an art exhibit of the Stations of the Cross. They were new paintings created just for this exhibit. My husband painted four of the pieces in it. Some of the paintings were realistic like Jesus hanging on the cross, but others were abstract. Jesus's betrayal was represented by what looked like a black and blue cloud with a sliver of copper. As I stared at it asking the Holy Spirit for insight, I began to feel betrayal through it and experience God's hurt and heart in that situation. God spoke through all the images—painted by regular people—in profound and personal ways. We miss out on a lot when we don't use our imagination to experience God. Don't be afraid of your imagination. Submit it to God and see how He wants to use it to meet you.

The Exchange

OUR GOD IS A GOD OF EXCHANGES. Jesus traded places with us by taking our sin and giving us His righteousness. Paul talks often of taking off one thing and putting on something else. For example, he says we should take off foolish talk, and put on thankfulness to God (Eph. 5:4). Stop stealing and do something lifegiving with your hands (Eph. 4:28). Don't think like the world, but let God transform the way you think (Rom. 12:2). Don't let evil conquer you, but overcome evil with good (Rom. 12:21). When we give our negative thoughts and beliefs to God, He doesn't leave us empty-handed. He tells us to leave our old harmful ways behind and invites us to step into a better, more fulfilling way to live.

Throughout the exercises in this book, we will talk about lies we believe. Much like the serpent lied to Eve in the garden, Satan lies to us about who God is and who we are. Most of the time we don't even realize that destructive beliefs are behind our thoughts controlling how we act and feel. In psychology, it's taught that beliefs dictate thoughts and actions, then emotions follow. If we want to change patterns in our lives, we must become aware of the beliefs that are driving our thoughts and actions. Experiencing God requires a willingness to be honest about what's in our hearts. It requires paying attention to emotions and finding out what beliefs are behind them. As we discover lies we believe, then God will be able to bring healing to our hearts.

Let's not forget, I said this is an exchange. It's not enough just to get rid of a lie; we must have the truth to replace it. The exercises will often instruct you to give the lies to God and ask Him to tell you what is true in place of them. God doesn't expect us to live empty-handed. He always has something better to give when we trade in the lies we've believed. And what He gives is so much better!

God gives amazing gifts in this process of exchange. Sometimes He says a sweet word. Other times He will show you a picture that has significant meaning for you. Whatever it is, it will be just what you need in the moment. For example, in one prayer session, I gave God a belief that I was inadequate. In exchange, He showed me myself wearing a beautiful white gown with jewels. The words "dignity and grace" came to mind with it. He was showing me who He says I am. When those feelings of inadequacy return, I return to that image of the lovely dress to remember what is true.

In a prayer time, my husband received a sword after years of believing He was defenseless. One friend received a simple, but profound look from Jesus while visiting an old memory in prayer. It communicated to her assurance of God's presence in that situation, and vanquished a lie she'd been believing about herself. His gifts are powerful, and He has so many for you if you are willing to discover and let go of the lies you believe.

This is the renewing of your mind that Paul mentions in Romans 12:2. This is the battle that is necessary in order to gain the freedom, healing, and peace God has for us. Claiming God's truths is the most significant task of walking out the Christian life. We can know them, but if we don't put them into action by releasing our old ways and receiving His new ways, our lives will never reflect the goodness and power of the Gospel.

Replacing lies with truth was a key tool that my husband and I learned on this journey. In fact, we came to understand that the lies we believed were a major cause of the crisis we experienced. At last mention, I was working at a well-known venue as a wedding coordinator. During that time, God was increasing my personal, mental, and emotional capacity. He was also giving me an opportunity to discover more about myself. It was an amazing time, but there was also a lot of difficulty. The healing was happening because God was exposing the lies I believed about myself.

It's difficult to find false beliefs because they're so familiar. They've been a part of our thinking for so long that they are "normal." We are so used to them, and oftentimes we don't know what we'd do without them. He took the lies and gave me lovely gifts in exchange. The best gift is that over the years, my life changed! All of my relationships improved. I began to understand people differently and I had more patience for them. I was less sensitive to offense and perceiving less offense from others. My marriage benefited with better communication and more grace. Our kids benefited because I was happier and could help them to recognize their lies and trade them for truth. I came to a place of greater peace. There are still lies, but they aren't tripping me up quite as often. When they do, I know how to bring them to Jesus for healing.

When I look back on those five years, I'm confident that it was all worth it. They were some of the most miserable times in my life, but they were also the most fruitful. I got to see God in ways that I wouldn't have otherwise. I got to see Him work on my behalf, hear Him speak to my heart, and be healed by His Spirit. He truly is a mighty God, and I have seen it and experienced it for myself. I am confident of His deep love for me and His desire to work in and through my life.

Everything I experienced is also God's heart for you. You can experience God in the same kind of life-changing ways no matter what your circumstances. It has nothing to do with you or me being good enough or getting something "right." It has everything to do with God's heart and His ability to meet you and love you. It's up to you to decide if you want it. Do you want to encounter the God who made you and loves you? Are you willing to be changed by Him?

Getting Started

WE CAN'T MAKE GOD SPEAK, but we can position ourselves to be able to hear. The first thing to do is set aside time and space free of distraction to sit with Him. Stillness, silence, and solitude are necessary to find God. It means being willing to create space in your life and heart to meet God. Then, it's important to be still long enough to hear His response to you. Being still is not difficult, but it's not natural either. It takes practice to learn to quiet our busy minds and focus our attention on God.

Our lives are often set up in a way that makes creating space difficult. Our culture of distraction keeps our thinking fragmented. Just sitting at my computer trying to write, I feel distractions all around me, fighting for my attention. I'm sure you know what I mean. I can also see that just as much distraction comes from within me. My mind is all over the place. I reach for my phone for no reason. I click a different tab on the computer. I get up from the computer to check something else, then grab my phone again. My attention span is so much shorter than it used to be. I've let the culture of urgency shape me. One way to fight against this is by sitting still in God's presence. Clearly, I'm not doing it enough. Between the busyness of everyday life, the distraction of our devices, and our instant gratification culture, it's no wonder that we can't be still. We don't even know how. But it is possible and setting aside guarded time in a quiet space is the first step.

Once you're in this time and space you've set aside, there is often internal resistance that arises. You will remember the lists that haven't been completed, or the nagging needs at work, or the many times you've failed before. It might feel impossible to sit there doing what feels like nothing. Your mind may not want to surrender control. Pay attention to any resistance you feel. Resistance is a sub-conscious avoidance of something. Ask yourself what's causing the resistance you feel. Is there something deeper you're afraid of or avoiding? Don't condemn yourself for the resistance. It's helpful to reveal beliefs working within you.

One of my favorite quotes is from the novel *Sensible Shoes* by Sharon Garlough Brown. The professor urges his students: "Linger with what provokes you."[1] We can learn more from what stirs us than from anything comfortable or easy. As you sit in stillness and silence, every time a distraction comes up, examine it, then hand it over to Jesus. Anytime something irritates you, pay attention to it. Talk to Jesus about it. Invite Him to be a part of all of these things rather than trying to figure it all out before you go to Him.

Here are some practical tips for stillness. Leave your phone in another room. Get into a comfortable position and set your gaze on Jesus (Heb. 12:2). Picture yourself with Him. Don't talk, just be in His presence. Let your attitude and posture communicate that you are surrendering yourself to Him because you know that you can't fix yourself.

GETTING STARTED

You don't even know what you need most of the time. You only know that you need *Him* to transform you.

I suggest beginning each exercise with at least five minutes of silence to let your mind unwind and slow down. It can seem boring and fruitless at the beginning, but the more you practice it, the more refreshing it will become. I usually leave times of silence and stillness feeling like I have more emotional and mental space than I did before. The time realigns me for my life. Then, approach the exercise from this Spirit-filled place of peace.

There are forty exercises within this book. It would be good to start with a plan, but I'm not going to give it to you. You can do one exercise a day or one exercise every other day. Set a pace that works for you—one that allows you to realistically get through them all. If an exercise is particularly relevant for you and God is really speaking, you might be able to meet God in it every day for a week. It's important to push through when the work feels stagnant, because those days always come. Be sure to give yourself adequate time to do each exercise. You need at least 30 minutes to settle in and have space to hear from God. Be gracious with yourself, but persevere, and you will see God move. The important thing is to keep seeking, asking, and knocking until you encounter God. He promises that if you seek, ask, and knock, He will answer.

Each exercise contains verses to contemplate and questions for you to ask yourself and to ask God. This is not a daily reading to check off your to-do list. In each exercise, I offer some Spirit-led insights to consider as you approach the questions. The questions are designed to invite God into your heart so you can see what's really there and He can heal it.

As you approach the questions, invite the Holy Spirit to lead you. The questions are a guide to help you encounter God. If God shows up for you in every question I have written, then I praise the Lord for His

Encounter

grace. But if a question isn't helping you, consider how you could reword it to fit you, or move onto the next one. You might do the first question in an exercise, and then the Holy Spirit might lead you to different questions from those that are written here. Sometimes you may need to sit with a question for a while or come back to it at a later time. There are times that I've asked God a question in the morning and not gotten answers until the next day. Sometimes God is mysterious!

During this journey, it's important to start paying attention to thoughts and emotions that stir within you as you go about your days. *Pay attention to what you're paying attention to.* Where are you focusing your mind and energies? What are you feeling and thinking throughout your day? What provokes you? Feelings are indicators of deeper things going on. When you recognize these movements within, ask yourself when they started and what triggered them. Why do you feel that way? For example, if you're feeling anxious, consider when did you start feeling it today and what happened to prompt it? If you're feeling annoyed or irritated, it's likely that your feelings are hurt. Think about what you're feeling underneath the annoyance, what caused it and what does it cause you to think about yourself. It will also be helpful to journal the observations you make. You will learn so much about yourself and the beliefs that drive you. Paying attention will help you answer the questions in the exercises by making you more aware of yourself. It will help you get to your heart so you can connect with God's heart.

Many times, the event that upset or worried you isn't the real issue. This provocation points to deeper beliefs and wounds within you. God is using whatever situation provoked you to show you something that's in your heart. Imagine a young girl who hears her parents argue a lot. In order to avoid the conflict, she goes to her room and hides any time they start yelling. When she's old enough to leave the house, she's thrilled

GETTING STARTED

because now she doesn't have to witness their arguments. Fast forward twenty years to her own marriage. Any time conflict arises between her and her husband, she wants to withdraw or just leave the house. She doesn't have the tools to handle conflict and she doesn't realize that her response is learned behavior from her childhood. While hiding in conflict helped her as a child, it's hurting her as an adult. Now she needs to engage with her husband in conflict to be able to grow the relationship.

Curt Thompson states in *Anatomy of the Soul* that 80 percent of emotional conflict between couples is caused by learned behaviors that were established before the couple knew each other.[2] That means that *the thing you're upset about is not actually the thing you're upset about.* This is why it's so important to pay attention.

The most important element is your desire to meet your God. He will always respond to your authentic desire to know Him more and be known by Him. My hope is that these exercises provide a way for you to experience more of God and His great love for you, and in doing so that you will find greater trust, greater freedom, and as Paul says, that "your roots will grow down into God's love and keep you strong."

Many blessings to you on your journey. I pray that you will meet God in ways you never knew possible. I pray that you will grow in faith and strengthen your foundation in God's love so that you are able to be the person He made you to be and walk confidently in the good works He designed for you to do (Eph.2:10).

Here is a simple prayer to start you on your journey of experiencing God:

> O Lord, my God, I long to experience Your great love. I know You to be a God of grace, slow to anger, and filled with unfailing love. I've heard of how You delight in Your people, knit them together, and know the number of hairs on their

heads. I want to know that this is true of me too.

As Paul said, I want to know how deep, high, long, and wide Your love is for me. I know these things in my head, but I need them to touch my heart. I have no real understanding of what it means to be loved by the God of the universe, the Maker of heaven and earth. I want to know more of Your great love for me.

I need this. I need to know what Your love and care look like in my life.

Give me eyes to see You, ears to hear You, and the ability to experience You at a deeper level. Speak to me so I can know You better.

I surrender my heart to You, trusting that because You made my heart and understand it, You will gently meet me in it.

Please come close to me.

I'm listening.

Part II
The Experience

Be Still and Know

"Be still, and know that I am God."
Ps. 46:10 NLT

"The Lord will fight for you; you need only to be still."
Ex. 14:14 NIV

SINCE WE DISCUSSED the importance of stillness in encountering God, it seems fitting to begin with an exercise to practice it.

Hearing the word "stillness" used to make me squirm. Just thinking about it made me want to fidget. I've always had a hard time being still, in both mind and body. My husband has frequently told me that I need a hobby like knitting in order to put that busy energy into something productive. I didn't learn to knit. It was much too difficult. But I decided that stillness was worth the effort, so with much practice, I eventually learned to be still in mind and body. All of that fidgeting and squirming was evidence of how badly I needed this discipline. It has been a saving grace for me over the years. It's a guaranteed way for me to find peace when I'm feeling anxious and rest when I'm wound too tightly.

Stillness is a multifaceted tool. It's a way to be with God. It's a way to declutter your mind. It's a reminder that you are not the god of your life, and that there is One who is or wants to be. Stillness counters the busyness and anxiety of life so we don't spin out of control. This practice will benefit you throughout the rest of the exercises, but more importantly the rest of your life.

Stillness isn't easy. It takes practice. It involves ceasing activity in your body and in your mind, but it isn't mindless meditation. It's a posture of surrendering yourself before Jesus and inviting Him to transform you because you can't transform yourself. During this time, it's important to keep your eyes fixed on Him, but let your words be few (Ecc. 5:2).

When you first practice stillness, your mind will likely be busy and scattered. Persevere. Sit still long enough for it to quiet. We rarely stop long enough for our thoughts to speak to us, so when they have the chance, they're excited to be heard. Obviously, we need to create more space in our lives to pay attention to our inner worlds. I take time to journal nearly every day to give my mind and thoughts an outlet. This makes my stillness time easier and has improved my sleep and anxiety levels. When a distraction comes to your mind, acknowledge it, then give it to Jesus. If there's anything you need to remember for later, ask Him to remind you. Another focus strategy is to use a word to refocus your attention on Jesus every time your mind strays—words like "breathe," "Abba," "Peace," "Jesus." You can also focus on your breathing to help calm down your mind.

As we discussed in the beginning of this book, "to know" means to have a personal, even intimate knowledge of something or someone through experience. In the verses above, God is inviting you to know Him. He is inviting you to remember who He is. He's inviting you to hand over your burdens because you trust Him. He is assuring you that if you *know*, personally and intimately, who He really is, you will be free to be still. When you can be still, you will be able to receive from Him.

He has so many good things to give you: rest, care, faith, wisdom, blessings, insight, and many more wonderful things that He knows you need. When you are free to be still, you will discover that He *knows* you, and you will feel seen and heard. You might even feel loved. When you do this, you will understand that He will fight for you and work on your behalf. Over time, you will become confident, through experience, that He is with you and He is for you in all things.

- Let's practice stillness. Close your eyes and quiet your mind. Imagine Jesus with you. Don't talk to Him, just be with Him. Notice where you are and how He responds to you.
- Once your mind settles, read these lines slowly, pausing between each line. Pay attention to any thoughts or emotions that rise up within you.

Be still and know that I am God.
Be still and know that I am.
Be still and know that I.
Be still and know.
Be still.
Be.

- Ask God what His heart is for you.
- What does it mean for you "to know" that He is God as the verse says? Ask God how He wants you to know Him.

Encounter

Prayer

Father, help me to be still in Your presence. I long to experience this "knowing" of You that leads to peace. I long to see You fight for me. Thank You that You are for me! Give me the grace to continually be still and let You be my God. In Jesus's name, amen.

Chosen

"You didn't choose me, but I chose you."
John 15:16a NIV

HAVE YOU EVER THOUGHT ABOUT HOW

you came to be a follower of Jesus? Do you believe that you chose to follow Jesus? Could you decide at any point to no longer follow Him if you wanted to?

We live in a very self-sufficient society. As Americans, we often believe that we are in control of our lives. While freedom and independence are gifts from God, He never intended for us to live independently from Him. He never wanted us to assume that we have control over our lives and destinies. This way of thinking leads us to wrong beliefs about God.

The truth is that God tracked you down, wooed your heart and mind, and led you to salvation through His Son. He made a way for your salvation. He called you to Himself (Rom. 1:6). The only part you played was to say "yes." If you're not yet a follower of Jesus, He is choosing you now. See Appendix A for a salvation prayer.

You have been chosen. Your parents didn't get to choose you, but God did. God saw all of your sin and brokenness and He still chose you. Why did He choose you? Because He wanted to. He likes you. When He looks at you, He sees everything He put in you: goodness, gifts, talents, calling. He sees the extra things you've picked up along the way. He sees who He made you to be whether you're walking in it or not. And God never stops choosing you.

You know that feeling when you visit a new church? It's awkward. You have to decide if you're going to go there. You have to join groups so people will get to know you. If you've been saved awhile, it can feel like you have to prove your maturity. (Or maybe that's just me?) They might decide that they don't like you. You might feel that you don't fit in. You have to do all the work to become a part of the congregation.

This is not how things are with God. He chooses you first. He invites you to come to Him. You're a part of His family before you meet anyone. You don't have to prove yourself or do the right things to be accepted. You just belong. You belong to the Maker of heaven and earth. You are on the side of Almighty God.

In moments of doubt, it's easy to conclude that you have deceived God or that He doesn't really know you. You might think there's no way He knows how badly you've messed things up. I want to assure you that God cannot be deceived. He knows all about you. He knows every detail of your heart, thoughts, and life—both good and bad. He *still* chose you because He *wants* you.

Oftentimes we aren't free in this truth because we aren't willing to forgive ourselves for our sins. God has already forgiven you, and if the Holy One can forgive you, surely you can forgive yourself. Embrace the truth that you are known and still chosen.

- Feel the significance of what it means to be one who is chosen. How might this change the way you think and feel about yourself? As you go about your day/week, remind yourself that you are chosen by God.
- Ask God to show you ways that He has pursued you.
- Ask God to show you where you are resistant to the truth that you are chosen. Consider why you feel the way you do. Talk to Him about your doubts and fears. What is His response to you?

Prayer

Lord, my Maker, in a world where people are often treated as expendable and replaceable, I want to believe that I am chosen by You. Thank You that Your ways are so different and so good. Thank You for choosing me! Weed out any beliefs in me that contradict this truth. Grow the roots of Your love deeper into my heart until I live out of this truth every day. May my knowing of You and belief in who You say I am cause me to live fully, give freely, and show Your Glory and Power to the world. In Jesus's name, amen.

Delight

"For the Lord your God is living among you.
He is a mighty savior.
He will take delight in you with gladness.
With his love, he will calm all your fears.
He will rejoice over you with joyful songs."
Zeph. 3:17 NLT

THIS IS A POPULAR VERSE that provides comforting imagery for many people. The words are used in many worship songs that we sing regularly in church. But if I'm honest with myself, for most of my Christian life, I questioned these truths because I didn't feel them or see them in my life. Can you relate?

Many people believe that God is disappointed with them, ashamed of them, or fed up with them. It's common to feel that we are just one mistake away from God's wrath. It's easy to consider difficulties, illness, or a wayward child as God punishing us, even though we aren't sure what for. I think a lot of people walk away from the faith because they can no longer bear the condemnation they feel. The good news is that God is not the one who is making them feel this way.

The images we carry of who God is severely affect what we are able to receive from Him. Our beliefs don't limit Him; they limit us and our ability to receive. Faith is essentially what we believe. Everything about Christianity is based on faith. "We live by faith, not by sight" (2 Cor. 5:7). Our beliefs don't determine who God is, but our beliefs limit who He can be for us. You can't receive something from God if you don't believe that He gives it. You can't receive from God if you consider Him to be a far-off Being who doesn't concern Himself with the details of your life. If you think of Him as a Judge, then you will experience Him through that lens. If you see Him as a disciplinarian or impotent bystander, then you will experience Him in those ways. You will get what you believe, because that's the lens through which you are seeing.

The images we carry of God are very important. If we want to experience Him differently, then we need to examine what we believe. Many times our images of God are wrong, especially if they lead us to think negatively of God or think God feels negatively toward us. Wrong images of God are lies. These lies keep us from being able to receive all the good that God has for us. If we want to stop living according to lies regarding who God is, then we must discover what we're believing and what is actually true. Fortunately, we aren't alone because we've been given the Holy Spirit who will tell us the truth about who God is (Jn. 15:26).

More good news is that even if you carry broken images of God, He is not upset that you misunderstand Him. He is longing for you to know His heart for you. He wants to expose the lies that bind you so you can more fully know Him and receive the gifts of His love.

DELIGHT

God's Word is filled with proclamations of His love for you and proclamations of His desire to throw everything else aside so He can show you that you are so important to Him. Even if you know that He loves you, it's easy to think that He is disinterested or that He loves you from afar. The truth is that God loves you up close and personal. He wants to shower you with His affection, care, joy, delight, and adoration. In order to more fully receive God's delight in you, slowly reread the verse from Zephaniah and consider the questions below.

- Read each sentence of the verse separately as though God is speaking it directly to you. (For example: I am with you. I am your Mighty Savior. I will calm your fears.) Soak in each promise. Pay attention if one part of this passage stands out to you more than the others. What does God want to tell you about Himself?

- What have you believed about God that is contrary to these verses? Take a minute to honestly examine what you really believe. There's no condemnation here. God wants you to know the truth and be free from any belief that's keeping you from Him. When you recognize any lies, hand them over to Him and ask Him what is true instead. He never leaves you empty-handed.

- Tell Him the thing you need most from Him. What is the area of promise where you feel lacking? Ask Him what is in the way of you seeing His provision here. Ask Him to show you who He is for you in this area.

Encounter

Prayer

Father, Son, Holy Spirit, thank You that You are my God and that You choose to live with me. It's difficult for me to imagine that You are so pleased with me and that You feel joy because of me. But I believe it! Remove any lies within me that tell me anything else. Remove all shame that seeks to hold me down. Those things are not from You, and I only want what You give me. I choose to live in the truth of Your joy, delight, and affection for me. In Jesus's name, amen.

Beloved

> "After His baptism, as Jesus came up out of the water,
> the heavens were opened and he saw the Spirit of God
> descending like a dove and settling on him.
> And a voice from heaven said, 'This is my dearly loved Son,
> who brings me great joy.'"
> Mt. 3:16–17 NLT

JESUS'S MINISTRY HASN'T YET BEGUN.

Jesus steps into the river and the heavens open above Him, and God the Father speaks this declaration over Him.

God is affirming Jesus's identity as the Father's Son. God is not declaring this because of Jesus's ability, accomplishments, knowledge, or success. God doesn't wait to see how well Jesus's ministry goes before declaring His love.

The Father's love for Jesus is unconditional, and Jesus needed to be standing firm in that in order to endure all that His ministry would require of Him. As God, this was unnecessary, but as a man, Jesus needed to know that His Father was pleased with Him.

As God's children, we all need to know God's unconditional love and delight in us. This gives us the confidence we need to move forward in our calling and purpose. We must be grounded in our identity in the Father in order to fully embrace the cup we are given in this life. It will give us peace, hope, and joy. It will infuse purpose and meaning into everything that we do.

These sweet affirmations and blessings belong to you too if you are saved by the blood of Jesus. God doesn't change, and He called us co-heirs with Christ. The main difference between The Father speaking this to Jesus and speaking it to us is that Jesus had no trouble receiving it because He understood God's perfect love. We, on the other hand, are prone to resisting God's love at every turn.

God declared this publicly over Jesus for the sake of the crowd. Jesus already knew this truth, but *you need to hear it and receive it for yourself.*

- Imagine God saying these words to you. His face and heart are turned toward you, desiring to assure you and affirm you. Feel His joy. Soak in it for three to four minutes before moving on to the other questions.[1]

"You are my dearly loved daughter (son), who brings me great joy."

- How does this affirmation make you feel?
- What doubts keep you from believing this passage? Talk to God about your doubts. Be honest. Listen for His response.
- If you doubt that it's for you, then look through Scripture at all the verses that speak of God's abundant, lavish, unfailing love

for you. Here are some to get started: Jn. 1:12; Heb. 12:2; Zeph. 3:17; Jn. 15:16; Ps. 37:37.

- Repeat this exercise regularly throughout the next few weeks and note how it changes your mindset and beliefs. Truth is powerful and the Word is living and active (Heb. 4:12).

Prayer

Dear God, thank You that I am Your beloved child. It's hard to comprehend that You want me and are pleased with me no matter what I do. But I want to believe it, God. Holy Spirit, move in me. Bring every part of me in alignment with Your Word and Your Truth. Expose the lies that are in the way. I want to be who You made me to be. Thank You that I don't have to perform to please You, but I just do because You love me and chose me. Thank You, that You have more for me. Please lead me into it. In Jesus's name, amen.

Intended

"Even before he made the world,
God loved us and chose us in Christ…"
Eph. 1:4

"The earth was formless and empty, and darkness covered the
deep waters. And the Spirit of God was hovering
over the surface of the waters."
Gen. 1:2

IMAGINE THE FORMLESS VOID that would become the earth. Then, imagine the Spirit of God hovering over the waters like we discussed earlier. What stands out to you?

Consider what God is thinking about as He hovers, or what the Trinity might be discussing as They look at the empty space. Do They joke with each other? Are They discussing what They would make? Are They waiting in silence as the ideas form among Them?

Encounter

During that time, one thing that God was thinking about was you and His love for you. He was thinking about the gifts and the calling that He would put in you. He thought of watching you grow through the stages of life and discovering all He has planned for you. It made Him happy to think of you. He adores you.

You are important to Him. You have great value to Him. He premeditated your creation. You were not just an impulsive action at the moment you were conceived. You're not an impulsive purchase in the checkout lane. You were on the list when the earth was just a figment of His imagination. He had already planned the details about your person and your life so you could do the things He made you for and be the person He made you to be.

Imagine the joy and delight on His face as He thinks of you even before He made the earth. This is His heart for you.

- Ask God: *What about me makes You happy?* Wait for an answer. Write down what He says. Drink in His precious words.
- Ask God: *Who do You say I am?* Drink in His truth and let it dispel every doubt and fear.
- Any doubts that may come up point to a lie you're believing about yourself or about God. Ask God what lies you're believing. Hand them over to God one at a time and ask Him what He wants to give you in exchange for them.

Prayer

Thank You that You loved me so much that You thought of me before You created the earth. I cannot fathom the depths of your love, but help me to see it as much as I'm able. I confess believing lies about myself and about You, God. I break agreement with the lies that I am _____ (fill in the blank with the lies you've been believing). I break agreement with the lies that You are _____ (fill in the blank with the lies you believe about God). I declare the truths that I am loved and was chosen by You. I am that special to You! In Jesus's name, amen.

Made With Care

"You...knit me together in my mother's womb. Thank you for making me so wonderfully complex! Your workmanship is marvelous—how well I know it!"
Ps. 139:14

"For we are God's masterpiece. He has created us anew in Christ Jesus, so we can do the good things he planned for us long ago."
Eph. 2:10

HAVE YOU EVER MADE SOMETHING with your own hands, like a scarf, a bookshelf, or a pie? Do you remember the sense of pride you felt when you had a finished product? Maybe you were able to give it as a gift or use it to decorate your house. Even if you knew your item wasn't perfect, it was special and unique because it was yours and you created it. You know how hard you worked, the places you encountered difficulty, special details you put into it, and where you overcame challenges.

God feels the same way about you. He's so proud of you because you are His intended creation. Like an expectant mother making a special blanket for her baby, God poured His love into you as He knit you together. He envisioned your life as He created you.

God is not deceived about you; He knows you're not perfect. He knows you lose your way, get distracted by the world, and mess things up. He's more aware of your shortcomings than you are, but He doesn't define you by them. He sees you through the righteousness Jesus gave you when you were saved. He is pleased with His workmanship!

The word "knitting" is significant here. Knitting takes time, effort, planning, and talent. It's a thoughtful practice that doesn't work well when rushed. Imagine the time God spent with you as He planned you and created you. He spent nine months working on you! He didn't take that long to create the whole earth and everything in it. This shows how invested He is in you, your life, and your care.

This verse is an opportunity to praise God for the way He made you. It's so easy to focus on the things you don't like about yourself. Instead, think about the good things about yourself. Think of the things that you like about yourself.

This is also an opportunity to become the best version of yourself. If you ask God, He will change and heal many things for you to become who He made you to be. We all know that there are ways we need to change. God wants to help you do that. Since He's the artist, He knows how to correct the problem and set it right. In the process, He will also give you a greater love of yourself to accept certain things that you've never liked before. God will honor your willingness to be who He made you to be. Don't be afraid to surrender yourself to the Great Artist who is so invested in your life.

- Praise God for the way He made you, for His care for you and intention as He knit you together. Thank Him for your body, your heart, your mind, your talents. Specifically list the things you like about yourself.

- Imagine Him creating you like an artist creates a work of art. Pick imagery that works for you. He could be painting to create you, or He could be knitting, baking, building with wood or Legos, or composing a symphony. Maybe He's drawing blueprints like an architect or designing you on elite computer software. Whatever appeals to you, latch onto that imagery. Ask God for a special picture or word that He has for you to remind you that you are His masterpiece.

- Look into God's face as you think of yourself as God's masterpiece. What do you see as you look at Him? How do you feel about being God's masterpiece? If it's difficult to accept, ask God to show you why.

- Tell Him about the parts of yourself that you don't like. Ask Him what He thinks of these things. Ask Him to change you or help you to accept those things. Take time to soak in His acceptance of you.

Prayer

Father God, thank You that I am fearfully and wonderfully made! It's hard to believe that I am Your masterpiece, but I want to believe; help my unbelief. Thank You for the time and thought You invested as you knit *(change to the verb you chose earlier)* me together. Help me to see myself the way You do

Encounter

and to value myself the way You do. I submit myself to Your hands. Please make me the best version of myself so I can be all that You made me to be. In Jesus's name, amen.

Child of God

"So you have not received a spirit that makes you fearful slaves. Instead, you received God's Spirit when he adopted you as his own children. Now we call him, 'Abba, Father.' For his Spirit joins with our spirit to affirm that we are God's children."
Rom. 8:15–16 NLT

"See how very much our Father loves us, for he calls us his children, and that is what we are!"
1 John 3:1 NLT

WHAT IS YOUR NAME? What do people call you? Perhaps there are nicknames or terms of endearment people have for you. Maybe you were called unkind names while growing up that you still hear in your mind. Did you know that according to the Bible, you are called a child of God? The Maker of heaven and earth is your Father.

We all had sinful parents who wounded us, so thinking about God as a parent can be difficult for many people. Most of us determine the type of father that God is based on our earthly fathers. We may know in our minds that God is different, but we may not truly believe it in our hearts. I hope that throughout this exercise, we can begin to separate our views of God from those of our parents, so that we can see what a great privilege it is to be considered Children of God.

Imagine the perfect parent. It can be the kind of parent you wanted as a kid, or the kind of parent that you want to be. If you are a parent, you understand how difficult it is and can see how your brokenness and selfishness prevent you from being the kind of parent you want to be. None of us will be a perfect parent. This shows us how much we need God to be our Perfect Parent.

Most of us desire a parent to pay attention to us in positive, affirming ways. We want them to understand what we're feeling and thinking and to shower us with affection and praise. We'd also like for them to be gentle, kind, and patient with us.

Now, imagine what it means to be a child. You are dependent, cared for, not able to provide for yourself. (You aren't helpless, but you can't control all of the things you'd like to.) Being a child also means that you're not alone. Children should have parents who are advocating for them and giving them wisdom and support to get through the trials of life. Doesn't that sound wonderful? A child also receives special things from his or her parents that no one else would be expected to provide: training, discipline, resources, an inheritance, blessing, platforms for success, naming, and identity just to name a few.

Do you need any of the things listed above? Your parents may have provided some of those things for you, or maybe none of them, but I'm guessing very few people received all of them. I'm not bashing parents; it's just the reality of life in a fallen world. The good news, and my point, is that God the Father is the perfect parent, and He wants to give you all of these things!

- Imagine yourself as a child and God as the perfect Father. How would you approach Him? What is the setting and your posture toward Him? Would you sit on His lap? Are you outside with Him? Are you doing something fun together? Are you tentative or comfortable with Him? How does He look at you?
- Examine any lies that come up about Him as Father or you as child. Break agreement with those lies and ask God to show you what's true instead.
- Tell God what you need from Him as your Father. Write down your requests so you can keep track as He provides. Ask Him if He'll give them to you and why He would do that.

Prayer

Father, thank You that You chose me to be Your child. Thank You that I'm not alone to figure out life on my own. You are with me and You help me every day. Give me eyes to see You as my Father. Remove any barriers to that reality. I want to rely on You and trust that You're caring for me as a good father cares for a child. Open up my awareness to receive what that could look like in my daily life. I surrender myself to Your care. I trust that You are a good Father. In Jesus's name, amen.

Presence

"You go before me and follow me.
You place your hand of blessing on my head."
Psalm 139:5 NLT

GOD IS CONSTANTLY SURROUNDING YOU.

Imagine the pillar of cloud by day and the fire by night from the story of the Exodus. That's who God is for you. He gives you protection and blessing. You're never alone and you're never without cover. God is with you.

Not only is He with you, but He's invested in your life. He's working on your behalf. He's not a distant God who's waiting around to see if you get everything right. He's surrounding you. He's closer than your breath. Alfred Lord Tennyson put it this way:

"Speak to him, thou, for He heareth
And spirit with spirit can meet.

Encounter

> Closer is He than breathing.
> And nearer than hands and feet."[1]

He's in the middle of the battle with you, holding you, empowering you, and fighting for you.

God wants to guide you in your life journey. This isn't a job He resents or gets tired of. He wants to protect you and bless you. He wants to show you which places you should go, which you should avoid, and where you should stay to rest and wait for Him (Pr. 3:6). He has all the intel on your past, present, and future (Ps. 139:16). He knows what you need before you need it.

Just like you, David knew what it's like to feel that God wasn't with him. He knew many unanswered prayers and seasons of fighting for his life. David chose to focus on what is true regardless of his circumstances. Many times we have to believe it in order to see it (2 Cor. 5:7).

When you're saved, God places His hand of blessing on your head. He is choosing you, calling you, and equipping you. His blessing includes all of the gifts that God gives His children: favor, grace, peace, joy, and abundant provision. He knows how to give good gifts to his children and He wants so many good things for you. Why does God do all of this? Because He loves you and *wants* to care for you.

Most of us don't feel or notice God's presence around us all the time. Part of this is because we aren't trained to recognize Him in these ways. But it's something we can develop and grow in. The exercises below are here to help you notice and nurture the presence of God in your life.

- Consider the truth of God's presence with you. Think through the past few days or weeks. Are you able to identify places where you saw Him? Some examples are a kind word or gesture from someone, the laugh of a child, a moment of peace, a chance to enjoy nature. Then, ask God to show you where He was with you. He loves to answer this prayer.

- Now that you see His presence, what does God's protection and blessing look like in your life? God's presence isn't benign. Consider things that didn't happen the way you wanted or things that did happen that you didn't expect.

- Take time now to think about the current difficulties you face. Imagine that God is walking in front of you as a guide and following behind you as a guard. Feel His blessing upon you. How does it feel and how does it change your perspective of your situation?

Prayer

Almighty God, I marvel that You care for me so much. Thank You for protecting me and blessing me. I see that You do all of this because You love me so much. Continue to let that truth sink into my heart. Help me to be mindful of You throughout my days, especially when I'm worried or afraid. Give me the courage to believe these truths. In Jesus's name, amen.

Unafraid

"For I have chosen you and will not throw you away.
Don't be afraid, for I am with you. Don't be discouraged,
for I am your God.
I will strengthen you and help you. I will hold you up
with my victorious right hand."
Isaiah 41: 9b–10 NLT

GOD'S GIFTS TO YOU and His calling on your life are irrevocable (Ro. 11:29). The purpose for which He has created you and the ways He has gifted you are a promise that cannot be broken. All of God's promises prove true (Ps. 18:30). If you are a follower of Jesus, He has chosen you and nothing will ever change that. It also means that you inherit all of the promises God made His people throughout the Bible. Before you believed, they didn't apply to you, but after you confess Jesus as your Savior, a wealth of resources becomes yours. If you are not saved and want to know more about how to receive Jesus as your Savior, see appendix A.

Encounter

These verses in Isaiah 41 declare a huge promise. It's one of the most significant promises that God offers to us for our time on earth. He says that we no longer need to be afraid. Did you hear that? You no longer have to fear anything in this world.

Fear is something we all deal with as humans. It often dominates our thoughts and our way of life. In America, we have whole industries built around trying to alleviate our fears. It's common to live life anticipating threats around every corner. Most of us don't realize that we let our fears dictate our lives. Maybe some of us know it, but we aren't sure how to live any other way. It seems practical, after all. What we don't realize is that these things of the world can do nothing to protect us or keep us safe. Most of the time, they just remind us to keep being afraid.

Why don't you have to be afraid? The Maker of heaven and earth is with you. The God who can hold back flood waters cares for you and never leaves you alone. The One who raised Christ from the dead lives in you and claims you as His own. He promises that He, the One who can give children victory over giants, will help you and hold you up.

Most of us don't believe this. We walk around with our fear like a shield, thinking it will protect us. It doesn't. Not only that, but your fear gives you anxiety, creates new fears, and isolates you. It leaves you paranoid of everything in your life. Fear causes you to draw irrational conclusions about what will protect you. It causes you to trust in things that have no ability to protect you, and the result is that you end up unprotected because you've chosen an idol over God. Fear lies to you and leads you astray.

In these verses, hear God's passion for you. He doesn't get anything out of it and He's not asking you for anything. He loves you and wants good things for you. He wants you to be free of the fear that has monopolized your life. All you have to do is begin to give the fear to Him and believe His promise to you. The God of the universe is promising you that He is with you and will keep you safe.

- Read the passage a few more times slowly and ask the Lord to highlight the parts He has for you today. Which promises resonate with your heart right now? Ask God what He wants to show you.
- Make a list of your fears. Then, one at a time, present each fear to God. Talk with Him about why you're afraid. Invite Him into this space with your fears. Ask Him to show you His heart and His care for you in regard to each fear. Ask Him what is true instead. When you're finished, burn the list. They aren't your fears any longer.
- Consider that He is your God. Notice the verse doesn't say that you are His, but instead that *He* is *your* God. What does this mean to you? Ask God what it means to Him. (After all, He said it!)

Prayer

Dear God, *my* God. You have given Yourself for me. Thank You that I don't have to be afraid anymore. Thank You that You are always with me and that You want to help me. Give me the grace to release my fears to You. Show me the ways that You protect me. I want to live my life as Your child, free from fear and filled with Your goodness. Thank You that Your ways are so much greater than my own. In Jesus's name, amen.

In the Waiting

"I will be glad and rejoice in your unfailing love, for you have seen my troubles, and you care about the anguish of my soul."
Psalm 31:7 NLT

DAVID WAS AWARE OF GOD'S LOVE because he knew from experience that God saw his troubles. David *experienced* that God cared for the anguish of his soul. It's easy to assume that God fixed David's situation and rescued him from the threats against him. We know this happened a lot for David, but many times David's prayers weren't answered right away, and neither are ours. There's often a time of tension as we wait for God to act on our behalf. It's in those times that we need to know that God sees our anguish and cares for us.

My husband dealt with debilitating anxiety and a panic disorder after our sixth child was born. It seemed to pop up out of nowhere one day with a panic attack and it didn't stop for five years. It was a horrible season. We felt helpless, afraid, and hopeless. God wasn't healing him in spite of much prayer and many different therapies. There were times that I gave up hope and tried to figure out how we would live if it were to be like this for the rest of our lives. I kept seeking God because He was the only hope I had. Anyone who has experienced a life-changing season like this knows that you don't often *feel* like God is with you. Most of the time you're just trying to keep your head above water.

I learned something very special during this season that I couldn't have learned any other way. I sought God often during this time because it was my habit and because I was desperate for His help. I remember many days, after my prayer and worship time, realizing that I felt better—more hopeful—even though nothing in my situation had changed. Something had changed within me, even though nothing had changed. In our circumstances, it was so clear that God was with me because He is the only One who can bring about a transformation of the heart in such difficulty. Only God can give hope when our circumstances haven't changed. I was able to claim that God saw my troubles and cared about the anguish of my soul. This allowed me to feel His love and continue persevering in the journey before me.

This is the true freedom we have in Christ. We can find hope, peace, joy, and love no matter our situation. We can also keep believing that God does hear us and will bring the change or the healing that we so desperately need.

If you are going through a difficult season and you're waiting for God to show up, I'm sorry for the pain you endure. I want to encourage you that God sees your pain and anguish. He cares for you. Don't give up hope. He has many gifts for you in this season of waiting. Seek Him so you too can experience God's care for the anguish of your soul.

- In the same way that we can't see good if we're focused on negativity, we also can't receive from God if our arms are full of something else. Ask God to show you what you are holding onto that may be preventing you from receiving from Him.

- Ask God to show you signs of His care in your life. Write them down. Keep looking for them throughout your day and week. Continually give thanks for these gifts. It will change your heart.

- Write a Psalm like David did. Share your troubles and fears. Then, rejoice because of who God is and that He sees you. These acts of faith and declaration will do much in your heart, and the Holy Spirit will meet you in this space of worship.

Prayer

Dear Jesus, You gave Your life for me. Thank You that You love me that much. I want to feel that You care about my troubles and anguish. When You don't answer me, it makes me feel that You don't care. I'm sorry that I'm so weak, so easily given to doubt. Thank You that You understand even my weaknesses and that You don't condemn me for them. Show me Your care in my life. Restore hope to me even if nothing changes. Thank You that You're with me even if I don't feel You. I know that You are a personal God, that You see me and hold me up. Give me grace to lay down anything that I'm holding onto that keeps me from receiving from You. I want to see You, know You, and receive all that You have for me. In Jesus's name, amen.

Rescue

> "I knew that you are a gracious and compassionate God,
> slow to anger and abounding in love,
> a God who relents from sending calamity."
> Jonah 4:2b NLT

> "They [the Israelites] refused to listen and failed to remember the miracles you performed among them. They became stiff-necked and in their rebellion appointed a leader in order to return to their slavery. But you are a forgiving God, gracious and compassionate, slow to anger and abounding in love. Therefore you did not desert them…"
> Neh. 9:17 NLT

MANY PEOPLE THINK OF GOD as an angry drill sergeant, an angry father, an angry boss, or an angry…you get the picture. Most of us carry a sense that we are a disappointment, an inconvenience, or an irritation to God, and that He is fed up with us. It might feel like your sins are too great for Him to forgive or that it's only a matter of time before He cuts you off for good. Google's English dictionary definition for "anger" is a strong feeling of annoyance, displeasure, or hostility. We can know the truth in our heads, but sometimes the space from our heads to our hearts is vast.

Consider the history of the Israelites. You could paraphrase their history like this: God did amazing things for them, then they forgot about Him and worshipped the gods of the surrounding nations. When the Israelites did evil in the Lord's sight, He allowed their enemies to overtake them, so that they might remember Him and turn back to Him. They became so miserable after years of oppression that they remembered their God and cried out to Him for help. In response to their call, He always answered them and came to their rescue. God did miracles among them so they couldn't deny it was Him. Then they enjoyed a season of peace. After a generation, it would start over again. This happens throughout the books of Judges, Kings, Nehemiah, through the silent period, and into the Gospels. Jesus was the final rescuer, and they even rejected Him (Jn. 1:11).

Here's the point: God is quick to forgive. He wasn't angry with His people when they walked away. He's not angry now. The suffering they endured wasn't a punishment, but the only way God could draw them back to Himself. He wanted them! He chose them! Peace and prosperity didn't keep them with Him, but suffering worked every time.

Sometimes we are as fickle as the Israelites. Sometimes we forget God, give into our fears, and seek other means of rescue and provision. What remains true is that God will *always* answer you when you turn to Him. It doesn't matter what you've done or how long you've been away. God doesn't hold a grudge. He isn't angry. He makes it a point to tell us that He is *slow to anger*.

What's even more powerful is that in addition to not being angry, He's also abounding in love for you. His love is so great that He will cause Himself pain in order to do what is best for humanity, to give us what we need. His focus is not on the ways we're wrong. He focuses on the good things He wants to give us and do in our lives. We just need to let go of the offenses we hold against ourselves.

Dear friend, there is nothing in your present, past, or future that will keep God from answering you and saving you. He doesn't see you as you deserve; He sees you only through the righteousness of Christ (2 Cor. 5:21). He sees you as holy and blameless. He is not angry with you. Ever. He has forgotten all of your sins and loves you more than you can imagine or understand!

- Reread these verses. How do they challenge your mental images of God? Identify the gap between how you think of God and who He says He is in these verses.
- In what ways have you let yourself slip away from God? Consider your heart, thoughts, and day-to-day life. Remember that there's no condemnation. Share it with God. Ask Him how to change and turn back to Him.
- Dwell on God's abounding love and compassion for you. Claim this as your truth today. How can it shape your view of yourself and your confidence as you live?

Prayer

My gracious God, I am constantly wandering away from You in thought, in word, and in deed. Thank You that You keep

Encounter

pursuing me and will always welcome me back in Your loving arms. Give me the grace to be humble. Give me the grace to see the ways I have forgotten You. I'm so glad that You're forgiving and abounding in love. Help me to experience Your love in such a way that I want to stay in Your loving gaze. In Jesus's name, amen.

Unfailing

"The Lord passed in front of Moses, calling out, 'Yahweh! The Lord! The God of compassion and mercy! I am slow to anger and filled with unfailing love and faithfulness.'"
Ex. 34:6 NLT

"When I said, 'My foot is slipping,' your unfailing love, Lord, supported me."
Ps. 94:18 NIV

YOU ARE LOVED WITH UNFAILING LOVE. You are loved by unfailing love. You are supported, secured, and rescued through unfailing love.

Unfailing love is used to describe God 121 times in the New Living Translation.[1] He chose it to describe Himself to Moses and the Israelites in the book of Exodus. It was important to Him that His people knew He loved them this much. He wants you to know that He loves you this much.

God isn't just loving; God *is* love. There is nothing in Him contrary to love. We get confused about what love is and what it should look like. I imagine that in ancient times they also struggled to understand God's love. Because of this common confusion, God wants to make sure we understand what His love looks like, and that it's different from the kind of love the world talks about. God qualifies His love as "unfailing" and surrounds his description with the words "compassion," "mercy," "slow to anger," and "faithful."

When God spoke to Moses, He wanted to make sure that Moses and the Israelites understood that their God was different. He wasn't like the false gods of the other nations. Those gods were temperamental, difficult to please, fickle, and demanded more than the people could give.

The God of Abraham, Isaac, and Jacob is different. He is unfailing love, quick to forgive, consistent, and personal.

Jesus made God's character clear for us when He chose to die to pay the price for our sins. He is a God who would give His life for His people. Paul explains it best in Rom. 5:8: "But God demonstrates his own love for us in this: While we were still sinners, Christ died for us." That's unfailing love!

According to the definition in my Bible, unfailing love means constant, everlasting, inexhaustible, sure.[2] I am desperate to know there's Someone who won't fail me. Are you? Do you need One who is constant and everlasting, with inexhaustible patience and love for you? This is who God is. As a believer, you are covered with His unfailing love. This is who God is for you. He can't be anything else.

- When you think about who God is for you, what characteristics come to mind? Where is unfailing love on the list? Talk to God about who you believe Him to be.

- Meditate on these verses about God as unfailing love. What does it mean about who God is and who He is for you? (Here are more if you want to dive deeper: Ps. 31:16; Ps. 33; Ps. 36:7; Ps. 44:26; Ps. 90:14; Ps. 107; 1 Jn. 4:16.)
- God's actions always support His character. He wants you to experience His love in tangible ways. Ask Him to show you where He was with you yesterday that you didn't notice. Be watching for His actions of love throughout your day and week.

Prayer

Jesus, thank You for giving Yourself for me. Help me to understand the depths of Your love. Thank You that Your love for me is unfailing, persistent, and faithful. Give me eyes to see Your unfailing love in tangible ways throughout my day and week. Give me grace to let myself be known by You as I come to know You more. In Jesus's name, amen.

Security

"I know the Lord is always with me. I will not be shaken,
for He is right beside me."
Ps. 16:8 NLT

"The Lord says, 'I will rescue those who love me. I will protect
those who trust in my name. When they call on me, I will answer;
I will be with them in trouble. I will rescue and honor them.'"
Ps. 91:14–15 NLT

I HAVE A FRIEND who says that Jesus always sits in the passenger seat of her car when she's driving. She's a realtor, so she drives a lot. She knows that God is with her. Are you aware that the Lord is always with you? He says that He is. He says that He is right beside you.

Throughout the Psalms, David is constantly crying out to God to save him. David was often running for his life; multiple groups of people wanted to kill him. In these uncertain times, amidst his doubts and fears,

Encounter

David always chose to trust that God would rescue him. He believed that God was with him in the midst of his difficulties and that God could and would keep him safe. David declared God's protection over his life. He boldly declared God's presence, security, and comfort for himself and for us. He made these declarations repeatedly throughout the Psalms, even as he expressed his fears and uncertainties.

We are not on the run or hiding in caves as David was, but most of us experience times of fear over our safety and well-being. For years, I told people, "I just don't feel safe." It wasn't about my physical safety or any tangible threat around me. Inside, I just felt that I didn't have what I needed. I was able to point to different circumstances at different times, but even as circumstances changed, the feeling never fully left me until I learned to trust God and experience Him as my refuge.

You might feel worried or afraid for lots of reasons. Maybe the money is running out before the month, your child is facing difficulties and you can't help, or you're waiting to get test results back from the doctor. Maybe you and your spouse are struggling to understand one another and the rift seems only to get bigger. Maybe the demand placed on you at work or at home seems to be beyond what you can give. The examples are endless. The common thread is a feeling of insecurity, a lack of safety, that runs deep within your being.

We all long for a measure of certainty in our lives. Certainty is what our Heavenly Father offers us—certainty that He is who He says He is, and He is holding you and protecting you through whatever you face.

As a child of God, you have nothing to fear even if the mountains are falling into the sea (Ps. 46:2). If there is a worldwide pandemic and you know people who have gotten sick and maybe even some who have died, you have nothing to fear (Ps. 91:5-6). You have the best protection available in the universe from the One who created it all. And He is right beside you! He promises to answer your cries, rescue you, and never leave your side. There are many times we don't see it, and there is often a time of waiting before the fulfillment. But like David, let's declare the truth and believe that God loves us this much.

- Read through the verses above in a personal manner as though God is speaking them to you. Pick the phrase(s) that speaks to the cry of your heart. Meditate on it. Let God speak it over you. Hear His heart for you. How do you feel?
- Imagine God right beside you wherever you are right now. How does it make you feel? What do you want to tell Him? Do it. Listen for His response to you.
- Consider a trial that you're facing in your life right now. How could it be different knowing and believing that He is right beside you?

Prayer

Dear Jesus, some days it feels like I'm free falling out of control and I'm helpless to stop it. I confess that most days my efforts aren't enough to keep the fear and insecurity at bay, but I see hope when I remember that You are with me. I feel solid ground beneath me when I remember that You hear me and You're right beside me. Thank You that You are a God who saves, and it is Your desire to save me over and over again. You won't let my troubles overtake me. Help me to feel Your close, comforting presence. May Your certainty overcome all of my insecurity and fear. In Jesus's name, amen.

Belonging

"You will be my people, and I will be your God."
Jer. 30:22 NLT

"You are my flock, the sheep of my pasture. You are my people,
and I am your God.
I, the Sovereign Lord, have spoken!"
Ez. 34:31 NLT

WHEN JESUS CALLED PEOPLE, they responded right away. The first disciples were fishermen, and when Jesus said, "Follow me," they didn't even finish what they were doing. They immediately left their nets and followed him (Mk. 1:16–18). Zacchaeus was a chief tax collector, despised by the Jews. He had such a great longing to see Jesus, that in spite of his wealthy status and rich clothing, he climbed up into a tree to get a better look (Lk. 19:1–10). The Bible doesn't tell us exactly why Zacchaeus was so desperate to see Jesus, but like the rest of us, I imagine that he wanted something more and hoped that even a sinner could be a part of it.

Belonging is a deep human need. We all long to be part of something bigger than ourselves. We want to feel that we matter and that we have something of value to contribute. Being included assures us that we are acceptable. In these verses, God is yelling from the rooftops that you belong to Him. He doesn't want you to doubt it.

A desire for belonging is the reason that people join gangs, clubs, even small groups. We hate being left out or lonely, but God didn't expect us to figure out how to fill that need. He created us with this need for belonging so He could meet it for us. He wanted us to belong to Him.

God gave us family so we could understand belonging and acceptance. That's why the Bible uses family language and imagery so often: we are His *children* and He's our *Father*. We're *adopted* into His *family*. When I talk about my family, I call them my people. I want my kids to know that they always have a place where they fit. I borrowed this idea. God did it first.

God speaks about us, His people, in a way that leaves no doubt that we belong with Him. It could even be considered possessive. But it's possessive in the best ways. God doesn't control us; He wants to give us security through His possessiveness. He also wants us to be possessive about Him. He wants us to know Him so personally that we can confidently, almost arrogantly say, "He is my God!" He also wants us to boldly claim His promises to us because He is our God.

It reminds me of Song of Songs 6:3: "I am my beloved's and my beloved is mine." This is the depth of connection that God wants to have with each of His people. He wants us to be secure and strengthened in the depths of our being because we know that we belong to Him. He is your God and you are His people.

By declaring that you belong to Him and with Him, God is giving you a platform of success to live your life. He's saying, "It's okay. You've got this because you're mine, and I'm with you. Be brave because I'm yours. You can live fully, take risks, love well, give a lot, and share freely because you belong to Me, and I belong to you."

The God of the universe wants to give you everything that He has, which is everything! All assurance, power, comfort, authority, provision, and victory are yours because He is your God. He wants to give you all things (Ro. 8:32). You belong to Him. You are acceptable, valuable, and deeply loved.

- Consider what it means for you that you belong to God and He belongs to you. What does it mean about His heart for you?

- What barriers rise up within you as you think about belonging to God? Talk with Him about them. Hand them to Jesus and ask what He wants to give you in exchange for them.

- What might it look like in your life to live possessively about God? What things could change for you?

Prayer

Almighty God, thank You that I belong to You. You claim me as Your own because You want me. I'm safe in Your care and embrace. Please remove all the barriers within me that keep me from living as though I'm Yours. Help me to grow in deeper intimacy with You. I want more of You in my life because You are my God. In Jesus's name, amen.

Carried

> "The eternal God is your refuge,
> and his everlasting arms are under you."
> Dt. 33:27 NLT

> "Praise the Lord; praise God our Savior!
> For each day he carries us in his arms."
> Ps. 68:19 NLT

IN CERTAIN SEASONS OF LIFE, I feel that there isn't enough of me to go around. Between the demands of marriage, kids, housework, a day job, and self-care, life is really full. Do you ever feel like you can't carry everything that is required of you? Do you ever wish someone would carry you?

Adults don't get carried very often. It usually implies injury or some kind of weakness. In fact, it sounds strange even to consider being carried. The hold is usually awkward for both people involved. It's also very close, intimate. There's no personal space if you're being carried, and it can feel invasive.

Children get carried. They snuggle in and enjoy the comfort and security of it. They don't think about feeling weak or personal space. My son is seven, and almost every night since he could talk he's asked to be carried upstairs to bed. Being carried communicates comfort, support, and help. It means that you're not alone. It means that there's someone there with you who is able to provide what you need.

When my husband and I were going through our seasons of difficulty that I discussed at the beginning of this book, there were days when it felt like the floor had been pulled out from under me. I remember experiencing a physical sensation of falling. These verses became a lifeline for me when I didn't know what else to pray. I would imagine God's arms under me, holding me and my family. Then, I could trust that we wouldn't fall. He was holding us, protecting us, caring for us even if there were times when it didn't seem like it. I took lots of walks and claimed these promises of God's goodness and provision. I knew He was carrying me. He still carries me. Our need to be carried through difficult times doesn't ever go away, and God is glad to do it.

What are you facing in life right now? Perhaps loneliness is threatening to overcome you. Maybe you face challenges that feel like taking on the rainforest with a pocketknife. Do your responsibilities feel like more than you can give? You've been seeking to be everything to everyone and you aren't sure who you are anymore, or your work feels futile, like an endless path to nowhere.

Whatever circumstances you face, are there times when it would be nice to be held? You spend much of your life trying to be strong and responsible. You take care of a job, family, ministries, and a yard. (I don't want to care about grass, but I do.) Whatever it is, there are people and things that rely on you. All. The. Time. Wouldn't it be nice to have someone on whom you can rely? Maybe Someone who knows exactly what you need while He holds the whole earth?

You need God's everlasting arms to hold you and support you so you can endure whatever you face. If you've always been the strong one in your family and relationships, this could be especially difficult. It can be scary to trust someone else to take care of you, especially if you were let down by those who were supposed to care for you. I encourage you to hang in the tension. Be honest about your fear and come to your Savior. He wants to meet you and help you if you will let Him.

- In what areas of your life would it help to know that God is holding you?
- Start with one of those areas and imagine God holding you. What does it feel like to be held? Ask God what He wants to say to you right now as He's holding you.
- Ask God, "Where have you been holding me that I have been resisting or just didn't see?" Tell Him how you feel about that and if you'd like Him to continue.

Prayer

Thank You, God, that Your everlasting arms are under me. I can't fall. I have Your help and support. I need You to carry me in these places: (list them). Give me the courage to look for and trust Your arms under me every day. Lead me so I know what decisions to make in these situations. In Jesus's name, amen.

Acceptable

"God saved you by his grace when you believed. And you can't take credit for this; it is a gift from God. Salvation is not a reward for the good things we have done, so none of us can boast about it."
Eph. 2:8–9 NLT

"I ask you again, does God give you the Holy Spirit and work miracles among you because you obey the law? Of course not! It is because you believe the message you heard about Christ. In the same way, 'Abraham believed God, and God counted him as righteous because of his faith.'"
Gal. 3:5–7

ARE YOU RUNNING on the accomplishment hamster wheel of life? Does it feel like you're going nowhere no matter how fast you run?

Our society encourages it. Everybody's doing it. We are praised for good behavior or called out and shamed if we mess up. We are wanted only when our actions fit other people's expectations. We perform, serve, self-punish, and compete in order to show that we are good enough.

God makes it very clear that we can't earn salvation. We don't need to do the "right" things or meet certain requirements to be acceptable to Him. It is all a gift. All we have to do is believe that Jesus is the Son of God and was raised from the dead (Jn. 6:29). Then, we are saved from all our sins—past, present, and future—for all eternity. Why does He do it? Remember John 3:16? "For God so loved the world that He gave..." God gives us this gift of salvation because He loves us. (If you want to know more about salvation, see Appendix A.)

Now take it a step further. Many of us can accept the gift of salvation, but then what? How do you continue to walk out your life with Jesus? The people in Galatia believed they had to earn it. They thought they had to work hard to prove that they were "good enough" to continue to be acceptable to God and walk in His favor and blessing. You and I often do the same thing.

I have a belief that I have to serve more to be acceptable to God. The irony is that I have six kids whom I homeschool, I work from home, and I'm writing a book. (If you're reading it now, it means that I managed to finish it!) I've been pregnant or nursing babies for ten years of my life. I don't have time for regular out-of-the-house service projects. But for some reason, I can't shake the feeling that I need to be doing *more*. That feeling has been there my whole life with Jesus. No matter what I plan to do or actually commit to, I end up feeling overworked and unavailable to my family and myself. It's never enough. I never feel like enough.

When I'm paying attention to the way I'm feeling in these moments, I'm aware that it's not about serving. It's about me trying to earn my keep. This is a good way to identify a false belief (a lie!). It feels like I can't do enough to make the burden go away and stay away. I can't do

ACCEPTABLE

enough to feel like I'm good enough for anyone or anything. Instead of working to make the feeling go away, I need to hand over this lie and be free of it. I bet God has a good gift to give me in exchange for it!

The truth is, you can't earn God's blessing. It's not possible. One who is born into sin can offer nothing to take it away. You can't earn God's acceptance, approval, favor, or grace. You don't have the ability. The good news is that you don't have to. You don't have to earn your keep.

So how does it happen? God does it for you. He already has the blessings for you, the favor for you, and the grace that you need. He chose you and He wants to give you all things. Just believe it! The only thing that can get in the way of receiving all that God wants to give you is unbelief (Heb. 11:6). If you don't believe that God freely gives you these things, then you won't be able to receive them. God does it all for you. He earned your way and freely gives you His acceptance and approval. Trust Him and rest in His gifts.

- How have you been seeking to prove yourself to God, people, the world? Ask God what will happen if you stop striving to be acceptable. If you're able, give God your striving. What does He have for you instead?

- What do you need God's help for in your life right now? Ask Him what He's already provided for you that you didn't realize you had. Ask Him to show you the way to move forward in it.

- Do you believe that God loves you this much that He would freely give you the things mentioned above? Talk to Him about any doubt or skepticism that rises within you. Ask Him what is in the way of you receiving from Him.

Encounter

Prayer

God, thank You that I don't have to earn the tools I need to live this life with You. Help me to receive the equipping You have already put into my life. Give me the grace to endure where You have me. Give me faith to wait on You and believe without seeing. Give me eyes to see Your hand at work on my behalf. Thank You that I'm enough for You! In Jesus's name, amen.

Seen

"Thereafter, Hagar used another name to refer to the Lord, who had spoken to her. She said, 'You are the God who sees me.'"
Gen. 16:13 NLT

"He made their hearts, so he understands everything they do."
Psalm 33:15 NLT

HAVE YOU EVER HAD A FRIEND or mentor who just "got" you? Or is there someone you easily connect with even if you haven't spoken in years. Maybe you have a friend who is quick to help you in your time of need. Maybe you've been aware of the lack of a person like this in your life and longed for someone to know you—someone you don't have to explain or defend yourself to because they know you so well. A friend who understands how you think and assumes the best of you in every situation, even conflict. Sounds amazing, doesn't it?

Encounter

This is how God sees you. He knows the depths of you. He understands your heart and your motives, and He doesn't criticize you. In fact, He longs for you to know how highly He thinks of you. He's filled with compassion toward you. With God, you don't have to struggle to be known. He sees you because He loves you.

Hagar was considered a nobody in her day. She was a slave and had no say over her life. In this verse in Genesis 16, she's in a desperate situation. She feels so desperate that even though she's pregnant, she runs away into the Middle East desert wilderness with no food or supplies. Even though in her society she was a nobody, the Most High God, as He was commonly known in Abraham's time, saw her and spoke to her. He saw her in her misery and His heart broke for her. She was His creation and He loved her desperately.

Not only did God show up for this foreign servant who worshipped false gods, but He also helped her. He gave her direction so she knew what to do next: "…return to your mistress and submit to her" (Gn. 16:9). It's difficult to know what she was thinking and feeling about this. In her cultural understanding, the gods did not condescend to humans, but this God was talking to her. The instructions weren't easy. I wouldn't want to go back into that abusive situation. Ultimately, we know she was changed because she chose to trust Almighty God who saw her in her time of distress and spoke to her. She did as He said, then God blessed her! He didn't just see her, speak to her, and give her direction. He gave her a blessing on top of it all!

How much more will He show up for you, a person saved by the blood of Jesus?

My friend, God sees you! He sees your heart, your mind, your pain, your trials, and your triumphs. He cares deeply about everything you carry. He understands why you think and feel the ways you do, because He is the One who made you. He understands you. You only need to turn to Him to hear His direction for you and His blessing for you. He will never force Himself upon you, even to give you good things. His love gives you a choice, and He waits patiently for you to come to Him (Is. 30:18).

- Think of a difficult situation you are facing. Feel your hurt, anger, and despair over it. Imagine yourself running away from it into the wilderness. Ask God where He is with you. Ask Him to show you that He sees you.

- Ask God to show you times in the past when He saw you in your pain. As memories come up, imagine the situations again, and ask Jesus where He was in those moments. Invite Him to speak to your heart as you imagine. It's healing to learn that He's always been there.

- Think of a specific situation you've been worried about lately. Say to God: "You made my heart. You know me better than anyone. What direction do You have for me in this? What blessing do You have for me?" He may not reveal it all right away, so pay attention over the days and weeks to come. Watch for the direction and blessing He has for you.

Prayer

Heavenly Father, thank You that You see me today. You understand the depths of my heart that I can't put into words. Please make Yourself known to me. Open my eyes to see the evidence of You all over my life. Show me that You see me. In Jesus's name, amen.

Rest

> "The Lord is my shepherd; I lack nothing.
> He makes me lie down in green pastures,
> He leads me beside quiet waters,
> He refreshes my soul."
> Ps. 23:1–3a NIV

WHAT BEAUTIFUL IMAGERY OF REST in Psalm 23. Doesn't that sound nice? Are you experiencing Jesus's refreshing in your life?

These verses signify rest and care. But in order to have rest, we must be able to trust that we're cared for. We must feel secure in order to rest. We can't rest if we're worried, afraid, or striving. Going without rest isn't an option. The human body is amazing, but it has its limits. This is why people have heart attacks and panic attacks. They aren't experiencing the rest for which they were designed, the rest that they need. We all need to know that if we sit out for a day, or a weekend, that our world will keep spinning.

Encounter

This is what Jesus has for you. He offers true rest that infuses you with hope, love, and peace. This kind of rest gives you everything you need to live a rich satisfying life and be the best version of yourself. You only need to be still long enough to receive it from your loving Savior.

Most of us are exhausted on the treadmill of life that seems to go nowhere. Even though we know we need rest, it's easy to get so caught up in busyness and activity, even entertainment, that we don't ever feel rested or refreshed. Many of us can't seem to get off the treadmill.

It's in this place where one of two things can happen. Either we figure out how to find rest, or God, in His wisdom and care, turns off the treadmill and *makes* us lie down.

God loves you so much that He will orchestrate your circumstances in a way that forces you to rest. It is only because of His love for you that He does this. He sees that the path you're on is leading to destruction, and He can't bear to watch you do that to yourself, so He intervenes. It could be drastic, or it could be subtle. God will use many situations to cause us to slow down if we aren't getting the message.

These kinds of situations are often unwanted, unexpected, and always unplanned. They can leave us feeling afraid, out of control, and helpless. This is what happened to my husband and me during his season of severe anxiety. For some people, God uses illness. For others, it could be a job loss. God used the pandemic of 2020 to cause most of the planet to slow down and rest.

I want to be clear that God doesn't cause the bad things. He only uses what's already there for our good. Because these situations are often difficult, it's easy to spend so much time resisting them that we don't notice what God has for us in them. Our instinct is to keep fighting for control, to make things go the way we want them to. But God is on the move, and He's working on your behalf. He's inviting you to let go, to trust Him, and to rest.

- Are you facing circumstances that could be designed by God to give you rest that you didn't know how to take for yourself? Tell Him how you feel. Ask Him to give you His perspective on your situation.
- Notice that in the verses, God is the One who does all the work. He makes, He leads, and He refreshes. Ask Him what your role is in your current situation.
- Imagine this refreshing for yourself. What would it look like for you? What needs to change in your life to get there? Ask God what good He has for you in this.

Prayer

Jesus, I long for that rest, but it is hard to let go of my sense of control. I can see that things need to change. Thank You for showing me that and desiring goodness for me. I see that You want me to be my true self. Give me the grace I need to let go and to trust You. I desperately want to rest. I trust that You're caring for me and my family. I want to believe. Please help my unbelief. In Jesus's name, amen.

Trading in Fear

"God did not give us a spirit that makes us afraid.
He gave us a spirit of power and love and self-control."
2 Tim. 1:7 ICB

"I have loved you, my people, with an everlasting love.
With unfailing love I have drawn you to myself."
Jer. 31:3 NLT

MY YOUNGEST SON has recently been afraid of sleeping alone. The strange part is that he doesn't sleep alone. His older brother sleeps in the bunk above him. But my youngest son says that he can't see anyone, so he feels alone. When fears like this come up with my kids, I always tell them, "Your feelings are real, but sometimes they lie to you."

Why are you afraid or worried today? When you feel afraid, do you ever take the time to stop and examine this feeling? Ask yourself, is it true? Why do I feel this way? It can be very revealing.

The interesting thing about our relationship with fear is that we believe it helps us. That's the reason we keep it around. Fear is actually a lot of work. It redirects our minds and our energy from the other things we should be focusing on and doing with our time. You know that feeling when you can't be present with your family or your work because you're so worried about something? It dominates your thoughts and consumes your energy. It's harmful to you, so why do you keep doing it? Part of you believes that it's helpful. You believe that it will protect you, or keep you aware, or prevent something bad from happening.

The way God talks about fear, I know that it never helps you. The Bible never says to pay attention to our fear. It only says do not be afraid. The above verse from 2 Timothy tells us why. Fear isn't from God, which means that it's from our enemy, and he doesn't have any good intentions for us. Fear can't protect you or help you. It's an erroneous conclusion. It's one of Satan's greatest weapons to fight against the children of God. Satan keeps many believers immobilized because of fear. My husband had a great revelation years ago. If we are afraid, it's from the enemy. That means that it can only be a lie, because Satan is the father of lies, so my fears are lying to me. Your fears are lying to you.

God doesn't want you to be afraid. It's a burden you weren't intended to carry. He loves you so much that He wants to take fear away from you so you can be free. The only requirement is that you have to let it go. He won't pry your fingers open to take it away. Many of us are angry because God won't remove our fears, but we're holding them with a death-grip even while we're asking Him to remove them. You have to let go. Then, you will be able to receive the good things that you've been longing for.

When you let go of your fear, God doesn't leave you empty-handed. Remember, our God is all about the exchange. According to the verse above, He has some really great things for you: power, love, and a sound mind. He wants to equip you for a life of victory. He takes your fear because He loves you. He gives you greater things because He loves you. It only takes eyes to see it.

If someone is willing and able to alleviate your fears, provide for you, and protect you, would you believe they love you? Anyone who invests in your well-being in any capacity must have some measure of love for you, otherwise it doesn't make sense that they would go to all that trouble. God doesn't just do one of these things I've listed. He does *all* of them for you. In fact, God cares for you better than you can care for yourself. Begin to receive all that your God has for you by letting go of your fears so you can receive more from Him.

- Considering the first verse, what are some ways you could view your fear differently?
- What does your fear reveal to you about who you are and what you lack?[1]
- Consider the Jeremiah verse. How could God's love change your fears if you let it? How might it change your perception of yourself, God, and the world? What's stopping you?

Prayer

Precious Jesus, thank You that You are serious about removing my fears. Thank You for being patient with me. I don't want to carry my fears anymore. I want to be free of them and trust You to take care of me. I see now how they've been hurting me and holding me back. Give me the grace to let go.

Encounter

Remind me continually to fix my eyes on You. Please hold me close. I need You here. In Jesus's name, amen.

From Fire to Freedom

"When you go through deep waters, I will be with you.
When you go through rivers of difficulty, you will not drown.
When you walk through the fire of oppression,
you will not be burned up; the flames will not consume you."
Isaiah 43:2 NLT

"God arms me with strength, and he makes my way perfect.
He makes me as surefooted as a deer, enabling me to stand on mountain heights."
Psalm 18:32–33 NLT

GOD DESIRES TO EQUIP YOU to handle the challenges of life. He doesn't often remove our challenges like we would prefer. Like Shadrack, Meshach, and Abednego in the fiery furnace, we must go through the trials of life. The three friends held firmly to their faith and believed that God was with them and would protect them, and they still had to be thrown into the furnace.

I'm sure they expected to die. The situation seemed that it couldn't go any other way. Until, suddenly, they were in the furnace looking around. They were amidst flame, but not being burned. The fire even removed the ropes that bound them. It made them more free. And in that furnace they had the opportunity to be in the company of their Savior and experience His mighty power. God changed a situation that seemed deadly to a mighty victory.

God wants to show you that you're an overcomer. You can't know that or be an overcomer if you've never needed to overcome anything. God doesn't create difficulties for us; life is ripe with them all by itself. If you trust Him, you too can come through the fire, gaining greater freedom, and having experienced the blessed company of your Savior in a way you couldn't have otherwise.

What does it mean to be an overcomer? It means that you face the obstacles in front of you with faith that your God is always with you and will not let the flames consume you. It means that you see Him come through for you because you waited on Him. You didn't try your own quick fix, but you waited for His better solution, even if you had to wait a little longer than you'd prefer.

The landscape of life can seem as uneven and craggy as the mountain heights. I don't often feel like a gazelle, but I want to. God promises that He has chosen a path for you that is tailored just for you and that He has equipped you to navigate it. As you trust Him, you will become so graceful that you won't even realize how uneven the path is.

God wants to make you stronger. He wants to show you how much capacity you have when you rely on Him. After my first week as a wedding coordinator, I was in tears and overwhelmed by the great detail of the job. I wanted to declare that I couldn't do it, but I knew that God had put me there, so instead of focusing on my doubts, I chose to trust that He would give me what I needed to do the work. For the first two months I felt clueless. I asked God to fill in my holes and give me what I needed every day. I believed that regardless of what I didn't know, I would have what I needed for that day and it would work out. It was a daily effort to put on this mindset of faith.

Then, one Saturday nearly three months in, I was setting up for a wedding and I realized I wasn't nervous anymore. I felt like I knew what I was doing and felt confident in my ability to do it. I marveled at how far I had come in that time. *God had increased my capacity.* I had learned to manage more than I knew was possible for me. God made me an overcomer by faith.

God wants to make you an overcomer. He wants to bring you through the fire that you're in. He wants to expand what you're capable of handling so you can live life to the fullest with strength and confidence. He wants you to be able to stand on the mountain heights without fear.

If He were to remove every difficulty, you would be weak and afraid, untried and ignorant. You would not know what you are capable of, nor if you have what life requires. But God in His love for you desires to empower you. The best part is that He does it with you. He sticks by your side, through your trials, and hands you the tools and weapons you need to overcome.

He's there in the furnace with you! If you continue to trust in Him, you will find that God's way is perfect, and you will encounter your Savior in a way you never have before.

- Remember a trial or difficulty from your past. Ask God how and where He was with you in it. Ask God in what ways He protected you, just like He protected Shadrack, Meshach, and Abednego.

Encounter

- In what ways did God equip you through that trial? In what ways were you stronger because of going through it? What does God want to show you about yourself from it?
- What is your mindset regarding your current trials? Slowly re-read the verses above asking God for the gifts He has for you to face your situation.

Prayer

Jesus, thank You that You can show up in the most unexpected places. Thank You for wanting to meet me and equip me for victory. Even when it doesn't make sense, I want to trust You. Please remove any barriers to my trust. Give me eyes to see the ways You're equipping me and strengthening me. I'm better because of You. Thank You for loving me and sticking with me. I know You will never give up on me. In Jesus's name, amen.

God With Us

"So the Word became human and made his home among us.
He was full of unfailing love and faithfulness."
Jn. 1:14 NLT

"This High Priest of ours understands our weaknesses,
for he faced all of the same testings we do, yet he did not sin."
Heb. 4:15 NLT

JESUS WAS FULLY MAN AND FULLY GOD.

He lived in all the fullness and weaknesses of a man and had access to all of the power and fullness of God. He was not limited in one in order to experience the fullness of the other. He was able to be both man and God simultaneously.

Paul says in Philippians 2 that Jesus left behind His divine privileges, not His divine nature, and chose to become human like us. In Hebrews 4:15 above, the author says that Jesus understands us. He understands us because He chose to come and live as a human, to experience our limitations. He chose to bind Himself with skin, time, and space, and to be placed under a curse.

In a time of prayer one Lenten season, I was imagining Jesus in handcuffs before Pilate. I was irate at the injustice of His situation. He had done nothing wrong and didn't deserve any of this horrible treatment. As I prayed, Jesus looked at me with flaming eyes, and He told me that this was His plan. As He looked at me, I understood that He was in control of the situation, and that it had to go this way. In that moment, as the fire blazed in His eyes, He was powerful, and I saw His divinity.

Then, the fire faded. He hung His head, winced in pain, and closed His eyes in exhaustion. My heart broke for Him. I imagined myself going to Him, giving Him water, and cleaning His wounds. In the vision, He received my ministrations and welcomed my comfort. In that moment, I saw His humanity.

Why would God become human like us? I'm sure there are many theological answers, and although they're important, that's not what I'm after. I want God's heart. Why would He do this for you and for me?

He could've come as God to dwell among us, but He didn't. He chose to become human and dwell among us. He chose to experience our weaknesses, temptations, sorrows, and pain. He wanted to show us that He was serious about His gift of salvation. He wanted to get dirty with us so we would trust Him. He wanted to be a God who could relate to His creation because He's so passionate about it. He wanted to meet us on our level to show us how great His love is for us.

You have a God who will not belittle your pain. You can believe that He understands and cares about your suffering. You have a God who knows the depths of your heart and the hurt you carry. You have a

God who doesn't blame you for them but understands why you feel the way you do (Ps. 33:15). What a comfort it is to know He understands me even when I don't understand myself!

He experienced everything you do—loneliness, fear, exhaustion, loss, pain. It may not have been the exact circumstance, but He can relate somehow. He never lost a child, but God knows the pain of children who reject Him and spend eternity away from Him. He may not have been financially burdened, but He knows the pain of a burden that feels too heavy to bear and feelings of lack (Mt. 8:20).

He wants to meet you where you are in the way that no one else can. Then, He wants to lift you out of the mud and set you on a rock (Ps. 40). All because He loves you so much. He can do this because He is fully man and fully God.

- What pain have you held away from God because you didn't think He could relate? Ask Him how He experienced something similar when He was on earth. What does He want to tell you about it?
- What does it mean to you that God became man and chose to live with us on earth? Think over your past week and ask God to show you the ways He was living among you.
- Ask God what all this means about His heart toward you.

Prayer

Jesus, thank You for meeting us in our humanity. Thank You for caring and understanding. That helps me have grace for myself in my weaknesses. I give You my pain, worries, and confusion. I trust that You will sort it out for me. There's nothing that You don't care about in my life and heart. What a Mighty God You are! Give me the eyes to see You living with me. In Jesus's name, amen.

Unburdened

"Then Jesus said, 'Come to me, all of you who are weary and carry heavy burdens, and I will give you rest. Take my yoke upon you. Let me teach you, because I am humble and gentle at heart, and you will find rest for your souls. For my yoke is easy to bear, and the burden I give you is light.'"
Mt. 11:28–30 NLT

THERE'S A POPULAR STORY in my husband's family about his sister's strong will when she was two years old. She had a new plastic shopping cart that she adored. She was determined to carry the cart up the staircase into their second-floor apartment all by herself. She wouldn't accept help even though she struggled. The cart was a burden that she didn't have to carry. Her parents offered to carry it for her many times, but she refused their help. If she would have let them, they could've made her life easier. Have you ever considered that Jesus wants to make your life easier?

Encounter

We tend to make life more difficult than it needs to be. We don't trust God's promises, and we choose to worry instead. We believe lies about God's character and lies about our value. We listen to the loud voices of fear around us. We carry heavy burdens, but Jesus is giving us a way out from under these weights that have become so familiar to us.

Sometimes our burdens seem reasonable, even though God tells us not to worry about anything (Mt. 6:25). During a season of financial difficulty, I worried. The bills were late, the mortgage was months overdue. I feared we would lose our house. We always had food, but beyond that, nothing was certain. This situation was difficult, and it seemed *reasonable* that I would worry. But, after all I had been through with God up to that point, I knew it was most important for me to trust Him. One of His many reminders to me was that "the righteous will live by faith" (Heb. 10:38). In fact, I had to guard my mind by avoiding well-meaning friends who might expect or encourage me to worry. It was clear that although it was reasonable according to the ways of the world, worry was not God's invitation for me. He wanted me to hand over the burden of worry and pick up His lighter burden of faith. By His grace I did it, and He blessed me with His provision at just the right time.

Jesus says His burden is light, which implies that there is a burden we *are* meant to carry. His burden is faith (Jn. 6:29). He asks us to trust Him, even when it's hard, even when we don't feel like it, even when it doesn't make sense. This is faith. Faith is a burden. It has weight and requires effort, but it's nothing compared to the weight of the burdens that are weighing you down now. Jesus wants to take all of those burdens from you. God told us to "cast our cares on Him" (1 Pt. 5:6). He wants to give you rest. He wants to teach you a better way to live so you can experience a freer life.

God wants to lighten your load. With a lighter load, your journey will be easier. If you know you're cared for, you don't have to worry, and your life will be easier. If you know that you're loved, you aren't afraid, and your life will be easier. If you can find joy in any situation because you know you're never alone, life will be easier. Jesus wants to make your life easier.

- Read the passage. What part stands out to you? Pay attention to any longings that are stirred up.
- Read it again. Ask God what He wants to show you regarding the things that stood out. What do they reveal about your heart and mind?
- Read it again. What does God want to tell you about your heart, desires, and longings?
- What burdens do you carry that God wants to take from you? Give them to Him. What does He want to give you in exchange for them?

Prayer

Jesus, thank You that Your burden is light. I'm tired of bearing the weight that the world has put on me and that I've put on myself. Give me the grace I need to let go of my burdens. I'm so comfortable with them that I'm not sure what I will do without them. Thank You for choosing me and being my God. Keep leading me on this journey with You. In Jesus's name, amen.

Unlimited

"Give all your worries and cares to God, for he cares about you."
1 Pt. 5:7 NLT

"He led me to a place of safety;
He rescued me because he delights in me."
Ps. 18:19 NLT

I'M SURE THAT NO ONE is out to kill you as David experienced. You're probably not hiding in caves to save your life. Most of us in America aren't being persecuted for our faith like Peter was dealing with. But that doesn't mean our circumstances don't require rescue from time to time. Do you ever find yourself in need of rescue?

It may be because life dealt you a bad hand, someone has wronged you, or because of your own poor choices. Maybe you were even doing what you believed God called you to do, but it didn't go the way you expected. Most of us are just living day-to-day, doing what we think is best, and then all of a sudden we're stuck. We are not in control of much in our lives. So much can happen that we can't anticipate, putting us in a position of needing rescue.

The thing about God is that He doesn't care why you need to be rescued. Psalm 107 tells of different groups of people who needed rescue for different reasons. When they cried out to the Lord, He came to their rescue. God doesn't go through a list of all the things you "should've" done differently. When Jesus died for your salvation, He died to take care of everything—your eternity, your problems, your health, your finances, whatever you need in this life. He didn't say, "Well, I've got eternity covered for you, but you're on your own for your health concerns until you get to heaven." No! He's with you now to fight your battles and rescue you from your enemies. And He loves you unconditionally through it all. He delights in you. He wants to take your worries and problems because He cares for you.

God isn't worried about His ability to rescue you or the number of times you need it. He's not impatient with you or asking why you can't figure things out. He wants to be there for you. He wants to show you what He can do for you. As long as you humble yourself before Him, He will rescue you over and over and over again. I know, because He's rescued me repeatedly. I often expect that He's had enough of me and won't do it again, but it doesn't happen. He's shown me that He's happy to come to my rescue whenever I need it.

It's easy for us to get so caught up in shame, self-condemnation, and fear that we don't want to ask God for help. Some of us might worry that God gets tired of hearing the same things over and over again. Or maybe you're worried that He won't meet your needs the way you want them met. Maybe you want to ask, but you've asked for things before, and they didn't happen; it seemed like He didn't show up for you. Pay attention to those thoughts and feelings. Those are the enemy's attempt to keep you away from God's goodness for you. Don't listen to them. Cry out to your God.

In 2009, we were affected by the economic depression. My husband was self-employed as a housepainter and the work dried up. We were unable to make our house payments. At the time, I was expecting our fourth child. We pursued every option we could think of to increase our income, but none of it was enough. We decided that my husband should return to teaching, so he looked for jobs all over the country. He had some promising leads, but nothing worked out. When September rolled around, the school year had started and he still didn't have a teaching job. Then, we got a notice that our house would soon be in a sheriff's sale.

This was obviously a difficult season in which we needed rescue. When I look back, I remember that we never gave up hope that God would come through for us. We each experienced moments of doubt and fear, but we always came back to God and His ability to provide. The sheriff's sale was a tough blow, but we planned to do what was necessary.

The next week, Mike happened to email an old friend about possible job opportunities where he worked. The friend didn't know of any jobs, but he invited our family of six to move from Ohio to Colorado to live with him and his family until we could get a job and get our feet under us again. We figured our options were an apartment in Ohio (if we could get a job), living with his parents or my parents, or an adventure in Colorado. Easy decision! To get there, one friend paid for a moving truck, and family members contributed for a hotel room and gas. It was an amazing adventure that is one of the highlights of our life thus far. God swept in like a white knight and rescued us! Not only that, but He never condemned us for getting in that situation. He was glad to save us, and then He led us to new and wonderful things.

Encounter

In these difficult seasons, the most important thing is to keep trusting that God will help you. We kept believing even when our situation was really bad. We didn't try to find our own way out. (Remember Abraham with Hagar in Genesis 16?) We waited for God's way. We trusted who He was and believed that He had good things for us, even though we didn't understand what He was doing and why He was taking so long. It's scary to give God your worries and cares. It's difficult to trust Him with the things closest to your heart. What if God doesn't work it out the way you want? What if God keeps you on the difficult path? This is true faith. When you position yourself so God is your only hope, you will see miracles happen.

It's easy to say that in hindsight after God has already come to your rescue. It's more difficult in the waiting, but it's most important to declare His faithfulness in the waiting. Your Mighty God wants to rescue you today. Sometimes it takes longer than you would like. Many times it doesn't make sense why He chooses to do things in the ways that He does, but I encourage you to persevere. Do what you can to put all your hope in God. Don't look for your own way out or your own temporary solution. Wait for your loving God to show up for you.

I believe that God makes you wait because He's using your circumstances to heal your heart. Healing your heart takes a lot longer than fixing your situation. Have you ever noticed that your areas of trial tend to strike deeply within you? They hit wounds of the past, they speak lies about your identity, and they feel like areas that will never change. God wants to meet you in the places of hurt related to your situation. Trust Him. Wait for Him. He cares for you. He delights in you. If you ask for bread, He will not give you a stone (Mt. 7:9). He is a good God, and He will come to your rescue if you wait on Him (Ps. 27:14).

While you wait, remember what is true about God and His love for you. He will never leave you or forsake you (Heb. 13:5). His ways are not your ways, because He knows things that you don't. Cling to what is good, right, and true while you wait (Phil. 4:8). Guard your mind and don't listen to the enemy's lies. Your God delights in you and He will rescue you!

- Sit with the verses for a few minutes. Imagine His delight in you. Create a mental picture if you need to. Ask Him about His desire to rescue you.

- Think about something you're waiting on in this season of life. Ask God what He plans for your heart in the waiting? Can you surrender your heart to Him to bring healing? If so, do so and note His response. If not, consider why not and talk to Him about it.

- Ask God what condemnation, shame, and fear you're carrying that is keeping you bound. Give these to Him. They don't belong to you (Rom. 8:1). What does God want to give you in exchange for them? Forgive yourself. God doesn't hold it against you, so why should you?

Prayer

Eternal God, You hold together the whole earth and You still care for the concerns on my heart. I need You to show me the way every day. Please meet me in this area (list your need) and give me eyes to see You and ears to hear Your voice. Thank You that You delight in me. Let that truth mold me into a trusting child who knows that he/she is adored. In Jesus's name, amen.

Perfect Love

"Love is patient, love is kind.
It does not envy, it does not boast, it is not proud.
It does not dishonor others, it is not self-seeking,
it is not easily angered, it keeps no record of wrongs.
Love does not delight in evil but rejoices with the truth.
It always protects, always trusts, always hopes, always perseveres.
Love never fails."
I Corinthians 13:4–8

THE FAMOUS LOVE PASSAGE. I couldn't do a book about love and not include this. Honestly, I am not drawn to this passage. It feels dry and impersonal. Every once in a while I use it to correct my behavior toward my husband, but this isn't a passage where I go to experience God.

The problem with this passage is that most people, like me, read it and feel pressure to become these things, so we work to achieve these qualities to make ourselves more loving. That's not bad, it's good to have standards, but I think it misses God's heart.

We must first receive something from God before we are able to give that thing to others. This is the idea behind 1 John 4:19: "We love because He loved us first." We can't be loving to others without first receiving it from our perfect Father.

I've had this book idea for over four years. I started it multiple times and had lots of notes, but I couldn't find the momentum to keep writing. I was plagued with feelings of insecurity and inadequacy. I didn't believe that I had something to offer that would matter to anyone. It wasn't until I went to a women's retreat and received a word about writing that everything changed. God told me that I was a writer, and He gave me a deadline for *this* book. The Holy Spirit burned away my insecurities and assured me that He had given me insight worth sharing. I couldn't finish the book on my own. I had to receive a commission from Him before I could do it.

We know that God is love (1 Jn. 4:8), but did you realize that God can't be anything but loving because it's who He is? He is not capable of being anything else, which means that everything He's done since the creation of the world until now is done with loving intention.

If this passage describes love, then we know God is all of these things. Consider the passage with "God" in place of the word "love."

God is patient, God is kind.
God does not envy, He does not boast, He is not proud.
God does not dishonor others, He is not self-seeking,
God is not easily angered, He keeps no record of wrongs.
God does not delight in evil but rejoices with the truth.
God always protects, always trusts, always hopes, always perseveres.
God never fails.

I can experience God in a passage like this! This is the kind of God I want to love and serve. We have a God who doesn't expect anything of us that He hasn't done Himself. And He always goes first.

God always gives us what He asks of us. He might say, "Just endure right now; here's endurance." Another example: "I need you to love this person, so here's love." "I need you to write; here's what you need to say." You're not expected to figure out what love is or to make yourself loving. God gives it all to you. You need only to position yourself to receive it from Him.

- Meditate on my interpretation of this passage replacing the word "love" with "God." What part of the passage stands out to you the most? Sit with it. Ask Him what He has for you in it.

- In what ways is this inconsistent with your image of God? Talk to Him about the parts you doubt or haven't experienced. Ask Him to reveal how your image of Him is connected to wounds and false beliefs.

- What are some things that you've been trying to do by the strength of your will that you haven't been able to make happen? What do you need to receive from God first? Ask God what He would like to give you.

Prayer

Jesus, thank You for being love to me. You have gone before me and prepared the way. I trust that You have done all that You're asking of me and that You'll give me the ability to do it. Help me to experience Your love for me in deeper ways. I

Encounter

wait expectantly with open arms to receive the gifts You want to give me so I can love myself and my neighbor better. In Jesus's name, amen.

Plans

"The Lord will work out his plans for my life—for your faithful
love, O Lord, endures forever.
Don't abandon me, for you made me."
Psalm 138:8 NLT

"'For I know the plans I have for you,' says the Lord.
'They are plans for good and not for disaster,
to give you a future and a hope.'"
Jer. 29:11 NLT

THE FUTURE IS SCARY for most people. Between retirement, current events, the economy, and health concerns, there's a lot that feels uncertain. The future can feel like a gaping hole of despair if you focus on all of the unknown factors.

Have you ever considered that God is holding your future?

God has plans for you. You've likely heard that before. This statement may chafe a little if you've experienced a lot of hardship in your life despite your best efforts. The reality is that even though God has plans for you, you have a choice in accepting them. You can choose to follow His plans for you, or not. His love gives you free will. He will never force His plans upon you. You aren't God's puppet. He *wants* you to *want* to partner with Him. You also aren't responsible to make it all happen yourself. When you partner with God, He will work on your behalf to bring His plans to fruition.

The plans that God has for your future are not about Him, they're about you. It's easy to believe that God has plans for us, but we often think that we will have to do something we dread in order to follow God. So we are hesistant to trust His plans, especially if there are certain things we really want.

I'd like to introduce a new thought—at least something that I didn't hear much in church. *God's plans for you align with His design of you.* If I were speaking, I would repeat it. *God's plans for you align with His design of you.* This means that God's plans for you include a life of joy and fulfillment doing what you love.

He is the One who designed you uniquely with talents, desires, and dreams. He's not cruel that He would give you a talent, but then not plan for you to use it. In fact, in times when you aren't able to do what you want, I think He's trying to help you discover talents you have that you aren't yet aware of. He wants you to use and enjoy all of the treasure He's put inside of you (Jn. 10:10). He wants His plans for you to benefit you, fulfill you, and even bring you joy. When you follow His plans, you will find that your work and talents also serve God and other people without a lot of extra effort or striving. It will just come as you live out of who you're made to be.

Not only is God holding your future, but He *cares* about your future. He wants you to have a *good* future. He wants you to have a good

PLANS

life filled with good things because you matter to Him. Doesn't it make sense that His care for you *must* include your future too?

His plans for you are consistent with His heart for you. Think of your own child or loved one and how much you want good things for him or her. It's the same with God. You are His child and He wants you to have good things for your present and your future. Unlike a human parent, God knows exactly what you need and what is best for you to make that happen while also tending your heart and making you the best version of yourself.

What about the times when the things that are happening in your life feel bad and don't seem like they're for your good? I don't have the answers, but I have a thought. There's a picture in my family room with a quote by Graham Cooke. It says, "God allows in His wisdom what He could prevent by His power." I don't think God causes the "bad" in our lives, but there is so much about this life that we don't understand. I don't understand much of the difficulty in my own life, but I've seen God use it. I've seen Him come through in powerful ways. And as I've chosen to trust Him, regardless of my circumstances, He changed me. Eventually, my circumstances changed too, but only after I surrendered and was willing to be changed. God is willing to risk your confusion, frustration, and anger against Him in order to get through to your heart. The significant thing is to choose to trust His character and His love for you, especially when things don't make sense.

God really is working in you, for you, and through you, to give you a hope and a future. He cares about your future because He loves you and you are precious to Him. I encourage you to ask Him about His heart for your future and decide to believe it.

Encounter

- Read the verses a few times. What thoughts, fears, or questions bubble up within you? Are these thoughts connected to any past experiences? Ask the Holy Spirit to reveal the beliefs you carry because of these experiences. Ask Him if they're true.

- In what areas of your life do you question God's plans for you? Tell Him these things. Be honest about how it feels and looks from your perspective. Ask Him to show you His perspective of your situation.

- Consider your dreams for your future. Ask God what His dreams are for you. What would it look like for you to choose to trust God with your future?

Prayer

God, thank You for caring about my future. Thank You that You're already in my future. I'm comforted knowing that I don't have to make things happen by myself, because You are with me working with me and for me. I marvel at the ways You consider every detail about me and what I need. I choose to trust You with my future. I choose to believe that You have good things for me. Guide me in Your paths. In Jesus's name, amen.

Power for the Moment

"For the Lord is a great God, a great King above all gods.
He holds in his hands the depths of the earth
and the mightiest mountains."
Ps. 95:3–4

"My help comes from the Lord, who made heaven and earth!"
Psalm 121:2

IN SIX DAYS God formed the universe. He made time stand still so the Israelites could defeat an enemy (Josh. 10:12–13). He put Himself into the womb of a young woman. He sustains all life on the planet (Col. 1) and knows every species of every creature that exists (Job 39) . The earth is His and everything in it (Ps. 24:1).

It is significant that God is the Creator of the earth. Being the creator of something gives one authority over it. The creator gets to determine the rules of order and the boundaries of the creation. If God isn't the creator of the earth, then it would mean that someone else is more powerful than He is (whoever did create the world), and that this force is outside of God's power and influence. If God isn't the creator of the earth, it means that He is limited. He would not have authority over all of creation and He would not know or be able to control the orders and laws that govern it. But God is the Creator and He does have knowledge of and authority over all the earth (Col. 1). You could say that He holds the whole world in His hands.

God is powerful and He is concerned with such large matters as these, and yet, He is also intimately involved in the lives of each of His people. He knows each one of His creations—people and creatures alike. He knows the number of hairs on *your* head. Wouldn't He then also care about the thoughts in it? He holds the mountains, but He is also aware of the small birds who perch there. He simultaneously manages the forces that hold the earth together while directing the steps of His people.

One day during my time with God, I was looking out my front window at our street and the houses on our street as I pondered Psalm 24:1. It says, "The earth is the Lord's and everything in it." As I did this, I saw a pink haze cover the whole street and all the houses. I understood it to be a kind of force field, showing me that God's presence and power were around me and that I could trust that He was actively holding all things. This gave me great peace that He was taking care of whatever was troubling me in that moment.

I find great comfort knowing that if He can take care of all the big things, then He can definitely manage my small things. I always find peace when I remember the vastness of who God is and what He does. There is nothing in my life or in your life that He doesn't see. He cares about you and all of your concerns, and He has the ability to do something about them.

- How do you feel about God being so powerful? If it gives you assurance, rest in that and thank Him for it. If it troubles you, consider why and talk to Him about it.
- Read all of Psalm 121, paying attention to what verses stand out to you.
- Read it again. Ask God to show you what He wants you to see in the passage.
- Read it one more time, asking for eyes to see God's love in the Psalm.
- How do you need God's power to come through for you right now? Considering what He just showed you in Psalm 121, what does He have for you in your situation?

Prayer

Father, You are so big. Thank You for defying my understanding. Thank You for the comfort You provide by the vastness of all You hold together. I need You to help me overcome the challenges that I face. I know I can do it with You. I trust that You're holding me and everything I will encounter. In Jesus's name, amen.

Joy

"Always work enthusiastically for the Lord,
for you know that nothing you do for the Lord is ever useless."
1 Cor. 15:58

HAVE YOU EVER had a job that you loved? What about a job that you hated?

God designed work to be fulfilling and fruitful for us. Work is intended to give us purpose. Work is designed to allow us to use our gifts, to do things that matter in our world, to participate in creation care with the Creator. But for most of us, work feels meaningless.

In Nazi concentration camps, the Nazis gave the prisoners meaningless work. With little food, the prisoners were required to do absurd jobs like moving piles of rocks repeatedly for no reason. Some had to dig holes one day just to fill them the next. It was hard, backbreaking work for people who were already weak and had no options. Some prisoners even had to bury the dead. Futile work in the extreme can kill the human spirit and even the desire to live. Proverbs says, "Hope deferred makes the heart sick" (13:12).

Fortunately, you aren't doing work as a means of torture, but work that feels meaningless can steal your hope, your joy, and your sense of purpose. This kind of work becomes a burden. It makes you feel like you just have to keep at it because it's the responsible thing to do, but there's no guarantee of fulfillment or joy. It's what needs to be done even though you're miserable while you're doing it. Oddly enough, although money is necessary and is often a high value, money is rarely enough to make a job meaningful.

The truth is you were made for more.

Are you ready for the good news? God cares about your work. He loves you so much that He wants to give your work meaning and purpose. Whether you're a slave, a factory worker, a middle manager, a CEO, or a homemaker, God wants to give your work meaning. He wants you to have the life and energy that He designed to come from work.

Here's His solution: do it for Him.

That's His answer. You don't need to get a new job. Begin to decide for yourself that you're working for God. Perform for Him. Seek to please Him. Look to Him for validation and reward. Talk to Him about your concerns and frustrations with your work. Ask Him what you can do to make your job better or to make a greater contribution. Ask Him for ways to encourage your coworkers.

God knows how hard life can be. He wants to make it better, so He says to each of us, "Whatever you do—diapers, cubicles, construction, or trash—do it for Me. I see you. I will bless you and reward you."

God promises that if you do your work for Him, He will give it meaning. Nothing you do for the Lord is ever useless. God cares about you regardless of what you do, and He wants to help you find a rich and satisfying life (John 10:10) in your work.

He also wants you to have joy in your work. Am I taking it too far? The world would tell us that we don't get to enjoy everything we have to do. But God has joy for us in all things. One of the fruits of the Spirit is joy, which means that when we live by the Spirit, He will show us how to have joy. You get to have purpose and joy in your work if you do it for the Lord.

- What is your view of work? Is there anything in your personal beliefs about work that makes it more difficult for you to enjoy it or find meaning in it?
- What work do you struggle to find meaning in? Commit this to God. Ask Him to show you meaning in it. (Wait for an answer now, and expect God to show you more as you go about your work this week.)
- Imagine God with you as you work. What does He see? Ask God about your work and what His heart is for you in it.

Prayer

Father, thank You that You want me to find meaning and joy in my work. I marvel at how You thought of everything. Show me the beliefs I have about work that make it harder than it needs to be. Make it clear if You want me to pursue different work or if You have gifts for me where I am. Give me eyes to see those gifts. Thank You that it isn't about the work, but it's about Your heart for me. You want me to be free to enjoy good work the way You designed it. Lead me to that, Lord. In Jesus's name, amen.

Enough

"Be strong and courageous! Do not be afraid or discouraged.
For the Lord your God is with you wherever you go."
Joshua 1:9 NLT

"No, do not be afraid...for the Lord your God is among you, and
he is a great and awesome God."
Dt. 7:21 NLT

FEAR, FEAR, FEAR. Are you tired of it yet? It's everywhere around you. The world and the enemy want you to be afraid. The enemy works tirelessly to reinforce your fears so you can't forget them or let go of them. But God has different plans for you.

We've talked about fear before, but it's such a big deal that it's worth doing again. God talked about it a lot, so we'll follow His example. In fact, the phrase "do not be afraid" is in the Bible 365 times. Telling, isn't it? God knows we need to be reminded constantly.

Encounter

God's instruction to not be afraid is intended to be a comfort, not a command. God isn't saying, "Geesh, will you just stop being afraid, you babies!" I think He's saying, "Because of who I am and how much I love, you don't have to be afraid anymore. I know it's hard for you to understand, but trust Me." He's telling us that this is a benefit available to us as His children. Most of us just haven't taken advantage of it.

Interestingly, God doesn't give 365 different reasons to not be afraid. He gives variations of one reason over and over again: "I am with you." If God wants to get peoples' attention throughout scripture, He usually repeats Himself two or three times. Given that this is the most repeated instruction in the Bible, I think God wants to be sure to get His point across. You don't need to be afraid because God is with you.

God is making us aware that the enemy's number one tactic against us is fear. If you're saved, Satan can't take you away from God. He can only try to make you ineffective for God's kingdom by keeping you focused on lies about God and about yourself. Bill Johnson, a senior leader at Bethel Church Redding, says, "Fear is agreeing with the enemy. Any time you believe a lie, you empower the liar."[1] You don't want to live that way. Neither do I. And quite frankly, I'm tired of being afraid. Aren't you tired of it? You have everything you need to be free of your fears once and for all. You have a God who is with you and who will take care of you in all things. It's time to embrace this reality for yourself.

- Reread the verses above a few times. Which promise stands out to you? Ask God why that promise is significant for you and what He wants to give you that specifically pertains to your life.

- Think of a situation or circumstance that repeatedly causes you to be afraid. Ask God to show you where He is with you in it. Imagine God in those places as He reveals them. Talk to God about your fear and ask Him to show you the truth. Ask Him what it means that He is with you in your situation.

- Imagine God telling you, "Do not be afraid, (insert your name). I am with you." Hear it repeatedly and sit with Him in this for awhile.

- Pay attention to any resistance that wells up within you. Look for the reasons that you believe the truth isn't true for you. Tell Him those reasons and ask Him what is true.

Prayer

Father, thank You that You want to take away all my fears. Thank You that You've given me everything that I need to be done with fear for good! You are big enough to take care of everything I've been afraid of. Show me how to be brave. Show me what I look like living courageously. Transform my mind so I see myself that way, living in Your strength. In Jesus's name, amen.

Royalty

"For he raised us from the dead along with Christ and seated us
with him in the heavenly realms because we are
united with Christ Jesus."
Eph. 2:6 NLT

"Because of Christ and our faith in him,
we can now come boldly and confidently into God's presence."
Eph. 3:12 NLT

I USED TO VIEW MYSELF as a poor, lost orphan child with holes in her clothes. It was a subconscious image. I didn't realize it was there until the Holy Spirit revealed it during an inner healing session. In the prayer time, I handed over this image of myself. God took it from me and gave me a beautiful ivory gown with jewels sewn on it. It was stunning! In the vision I understood that He wanted me to wear dignity and grace and that He was offering them to me. Every time I'm tempted to think poorly of myself, I remember that gown and remind myself that I am clothed with dignity and grace. Then, I seek to live through that lens.

Recently, my daughter was telling me some frustrations she's been feeling about her new dance studio. Most of the girls her age have been dancing for much longer than she has and are in more advanced classes. My daughter was feeling out of place and excluded when she was with them even though one of them is her best friend from school. My heart broke for her because I know that feeling.

I sought to comfort her and speak truth to her. It was clear to me as we talked that she *did* fit in with the other girls regardless of their dance experience. The biggest problem was that she didn't *believe* it, and her belief was causing the separation she felt.

Many times we let our insecurities keep us from asserting ourselves or from believing that we fit in. It requires a lot of self-awareness to recognize that we're believing lies about who we are. We often live and act as though those beliefs are true. The truth is that they're lies that are affecting our mindset and actions.

Is it time to change your mindset about who you are? Do you know who you are?

You are royalty. You are a beloved child of the King.

When you were saved, you were given a new identity in Christ. He gave you His righteousness and holiness. He declared that you are a new creation. You now carry the dignity of heaven.

I think of royalty as living boldly and unapologetically. I imagine an attitude that says, "This is who I am, and I'm proud of it." Royal figures walk and talk with authority and confidence. They posture themselves in a manner worthy of their positions. They aren't arrogant or belittling or even exclusive, but humble and kind toward those they encounter.

ROYALTY

It was said of Jesus in the Gospel of Mark, "The people were amazed at his teaching, for he taught with *real authority*" (emphasis mine). This is how we should be—confident and assured because we are backed by the Maker of the heavens.

Members of the royal court are allowed to have an audience with the king. In fact, they're related to him. They might have to request his attention or wait to be summoned, but most people in the kingdom would never be allowed to speak to the king.

Our God tells us what we must do to meet with Him. He says we can come boldly into His presence. Imagine Him on His throne in the middle of meeting with the angels. You have a need, so you go to Him. The angels guarding the door know that you're allowed to be there, so they don't stop you. You storm through the double doors without hesitation or apology. You interrupt the meeting and there is no rebuke. The King stops His meeting to hear you and answer you. You know what you've been given, and you're not afraid to walk in it.

Paul told us to "let our conduct fit the level we have already reached" (Ph. 3:16 CJB). God gives us great position and standing with Him so we can use them for His glory and our good. Believe who He says you are and live it!

Children of the King—princes or princesses—don't hang their heads in shame or hide in the back of the room. They don't sit around and wait for others to step up and do the work. They are bold and confident. They know the resources that back them and the power that goes with them. They have security in their position, so they are able to see beyond their own needs. In fact, they rarely consider their own needs because they trust they are met by the King. They walk with dignity and grace.

This is how you're meant to live. You have been chosen by God to be a part of His household. Paul says in Eph. 4:24 (CJB), "Clothe yourselves with the new nature created to be godly." This is not a burden that He's giving you. God doesn't seek to make life harder for us; this new way of life is a privilege, an honor, and a blessing.

Throw off everything that prevents you from believing the truth of who you are. No more shame, no more fear, no more timidity. You've been chosen. You belong. You are seated in heaven. It doesn't matter how much dance experience you have!

- What image have you been carrying about yourself? Compare it to the verse above. Is this who God says you are? If not, hand it over to Him and ask what He has for you instead.
- Start building a mindset of royalty. What do you need to throw off? How do you need to think of yourself differently?
- Imagine yourself as the one storming into the throne room with your requests. Boldly approach God with your requests. How does it feel?

Prayer

King of Kings, thank You for clothing me with dignity and grace. I want to live out of who You made me to be. Please gently expose the pain and inadequacies that have been defining my identity. Teach me what it means to walk as Your beloved child, holy and dearly loved. In Jesus's name, amen.

Nourished

"You cause grass to grow for the livestock
and plants for people to use.
You allow them to produce food from the earth—
wine to make them glad, olive oil to soothe their skin,
and bread to give them strength."
Ps. 104:14–15 NLT

"In the past he permitted all the nations to go their own ways, but he never left them without evidence of himself and his goodness. For instance, he sends you rain and good crops and gives you food and joyful hearts."
Act. 14:16–17 NLT

FOOD IS A FUNNY THING. It's a necessity, but it can be a luxury. It is an avenue both for sin and for worship. It can monopolize our thoughts, whether it's planning to feed a family every day or for weight management. We can begin to hate it as much as we love it. In all of your thinking about food, have you ever considered the significance of food to God?

I've heard many moms joke when their kids are hungry: "Didn't I just feed you yesterday?" It takes a lot of work and mental energy to plan menus, shop for groceries, and cook every day. I can't imagine how much more so in ancient times when people had to harvest their own grain, make their own flour, and then make the loaves of bread. When someone in the Bible prepared a meal for another, it's often mentioned that meal preparation began with killing the animal they planned to eat (Lk. 15:23). I don't know much about the process of slaughter to table, but it seems like it would take a really, really long time.

Food is discussed repeatedly throughout Scripture. In the beginning, God told Adam and Eve what food they could eat. God characterized the promised land as "a land flowing with milk and honey" (Ex. 3:8). While the Israelites wandered the wilderness, God provided them with manna and quail regularly. He mandated multiple festivals for His people that centered around food. Abraham and Gideon prepared meals for the angel of the Lord as an offering. Jesus made it a point to share meals with friends and sinners. The book of Acts mentions that the first church was intentional about sharing meals together (Act. 2:42). Jesus instructed us to remember His sacrifice with bread and wine. The Lord's Prayer asks for food, and Jesus did a miracle of multiplying food to feed the 5,000.

Food is important to God. Food is a means by which we interact with our Creator. It's a way to receive from Him as Provider and worship Him as our God. Food is a necessity of life that we often take for granted, but God wants it to be an accessible way for His people to encounter Him as well as a way for Him to show Himself to His people.

When you sit down to enjoy a meal with family and friends, you can experience God's goodness for you in tangible ways. If you allow Him, God will use food to meet you, fill you, and nourish you—physically and spiritually. Around the table with food is a place to share fellowship, laughter, joy, and praise. It's also intended to be a place where God is with you. He loves to provide for you and care for you.

In our very efficient, success-driven society, it's easy to take for granted all the food that is available to us all the time. There are grocery stores on every corner with more than we need. When food is so convenient, and we have the money to go get it any time whenever we want, it's easy to forget that every good thing comes from God. It's easy to forget that God provides the food at the grocery store.

How might our interaction with food change if we shift our mindsets to consider that the abundance of grocery stores is a sign of God's abundant provision for us? In fact, the provision of food could be described as extravagant and luxurious. Where I live, we are able to buy fruits and vegetables that are shipped from all over the world because we can't grow them in Ohio. This morning I ate a Texas grapefruit. My grandpa always said grapefruits from Texas are the best, and I agree. Every meal can become an opportunity to recognize God's care for us even when there are other prayers He hasn't yet answered.

With each meal, we can recognize food as a gift of God's faithfulness. We can choose to see the lavish love of a Father who wants to give good things to His children, and it's right there in front of you every day. You don't have to search for it, because it's all around you like love letters from God reminding you that He is with you and loves you.

Encounter

- Confess the ways you've de-valued food and taken it for granted. Thank Him for the abundance of food that you have and consume every day. Slowly reread the verses above. Ask God what He wants to show you about food.

- Consider your attitudes and relationship toward food. How much time do you spend thinking about it and why? Talk to God about all of it. Ask Him for a few ways you can start thinking about food differently. Write them down and incorporate them into your daily routines.

- Be intentional about planning a few meals as a means of enjoying fellowship with others and encountering God. How could you make it a time when you turn to God, hear from Him, and share with Him?

Prayer

Thank You, God, for providing so much food for me to eat. Open my eyes to see Your abundant daily provision for my care and nourishment. Change my view of food and show me how to use it to connect with You every day. Tell me things about Your heart for me every time I eat. Help me to elevate the act of eating from the mundane to the mystical, and may it make my mind and body healthier in the process. In Jesus's name, amen.

Memorials

"Those who are wise will take all this to heart;
they will see in our history the faithful love of the Lord."
Ps. 107:43 NLT

"But don't be afraid of them! Just remember what the Lord your
God did to Pharaoh and to all the land of Egypt."
Dt. 7:18 NLT

MEMORY IS POWERFUL. Memory shapes the way we live our lives. We can choose to dwell on the hurt of the past, or we can choose to dwell on the good of the past. Whichever we choose determines how we live in the present.

God tells us to remember His goodness and to let that propel us forward in faith. If we saw Him do mighty things before, we can trust that He will do them again when we are in need. In the meantime, it's important to cling to those past victories to encourage our faith while we're waiting for God now.

In one difficult season of our lives while we were waiting for God's provision, the kids and I built a memorial out of red Solo cups. We wrote on each cup a memory of God's provision from our past. Everyone took turns thinking of some that they remembered. Then, we taped the cups together into a pyramid. The process of remembering encouraged all of us and helped us to keep waiting faithfully for God to answer.

Remembering with God is also healing. We all carry the brokenness of our past hurts. It can be difficult to see how God was with you in the midst of traumatic circumstances, especially if they happened when you were a child. Looking back with God can heal those old wounds by showing you how Jesus was there with you then, and by hearing Him speak His heart to your heart now.

Between the ages of nine and fourteen I was lonely a lot. When I revisit that time in memories, God always shows me how He was with me even before I knew Him. He has given me very specific encounters with His love, grace, and protection as I have looked into the past. I have found healing and comfort in learning of His presence even though I couldn't see it at that time.

We build monuments by remembering as we look back over our lives. Pick out specific instances of God's faithfulness to you and give thanks for His constant love. Celebrate the good things He's done for you. His love is always there, even in the brokenness. Sometimes you just have to ask Him to help you see it. Look for times when you experienced protection, provision, comfort, surprises, and blessings. All good things come from God, so any of these good things are Him loving you. Remember these good things over and over and over again. These memories become monuments of God's love that will support your heart and faith throughout your life.

MEMORIALS

In more difficult memories, revisit them with God and ask Him where He was with you. He will show you that He was there even though you didn't know it. He is not bound by time, so He can heal wounds that happened at any time in your life. He can fix one horrible wound from fifteen years ago and it will have a snowball effect through your heart as that healing trickles through the annals of your past up into your present.

A good time to recall God's goodness is when difficulties come your way. It helps if there are already monuments that you can look back and see, but it's never too late to start building them. When I do this, I feel my heart swell with God's love in my history. Fear melts away and faith rises within me. I am assured that God loves me and is with me. Even if He doesn't do exactly what I want Him to do, I know that He will do what I need most and I will never be left alone.

God has always been with you, even when you didn't recognize Him. He has always loved you and sought to draw you to know Him. He made you because He wanted to enjoy a life-giving relationship with you similar to what He had with Adam and Eve in the garden. Now you get to choose to get to know Him, learn His heart for you, and recognize all that He's done to direct your paths.

Remembering isn't for God. He gets nothing out of it. It is for you. Remembering is to build your faith and to show you the truth of God's heart for you even when you can't feel it or see it in your present circumstance. God wants you to know that He has always been with you so that you will know that He will always be with you.

- Look back over your life. Start building monuments by remembering things that God has done for you. Write them down. Celebrate God's love and faithfulness to you throughout your past.

Encounter

- Remember one difficult memory in your past. Ask Jesus where He was with you in it. What is His response to you and the situation? Ask Him to change it for you. Imagine Him intervening and taking care of you.

- Is there any area of your life where your faith is wavering? Ask God to use this remembering to encourage your faith. Remember that He is a God who makes new things out of nothing (Rom. 4:17).

Prayer

I trust that You have always been with me, even when I didn't see it. You are my God, and You have been my God for all my days. Give me grace to see You in the most difficult memories that I can't yet revisit. Meet me in the places where I am still confused, where I feel that You failed to answer. You are my God, and I choose to trust You. Be close so I can feel You with me today as I remember. In Jesus's name, amen.

Surrounded

*"For his unfailing love toward those who fear him
is as great as the height of the heavens above the earth."*
Ps. 103:11 NLT

"So now I live with the confidence that there is nothing in the universe with the power to separate us from God's love. I'm convinced that his love will triumph over death, life's troubles, fallen angels, or dark rulers in the heavens. There is nothing in our present or future circumstances that can weaken his love. There is no power above us or beneath us—no power that could ever be found in the universe that can distance us from God's passionate love, which is lavished upon us through our Lord Jesus, the Anointed One!"
Romans 8:38–39 TPT

"I LOVE YOU INFINITY ZOOM ZOOM." This is how my younger boys and I say "I will always love you." It started when my husband and I were dating. I often said to him, "I love you bunches and bunches." (I was young and had poor communication skills.) So I started saying it to my kids when they were babies, and when they started talking, they would say it back. But my younger boys didn't like it and wanted a different phrase. This was their creation.

There are so many songs and sayings that seek to express love. I love you to the moon and back. I love you forever. I love you times infinity. I used to read a book to my older boys called *I Love You, Stinky Face*. My daughter had a book called *I Love You Through and Through*. One line in it said, "I love you as the sun loves the bright blue days." And remember the pop song "Ain't no Mountain High Enough"?

The words "I love you" are so overused in our culture that they seem meaningless. We have to get creative to show sincerity and intention. Sometimes language just seems to fall short, so we create analogies to express our feelings.

I don't think God is using figurative language here, although He is a poet. Psalm 33:5 says, "The unfailing love of the Lord fills the earth." I think in this instance it's literal. If God's love is as great as the height of the heavens above the earth, maybe this is a true measure. Everywhere we go, His love is there. This is supported in Psalm 139. Romans 8 is expressing thoroughly and literally that nothing can keep God from loving us. Paul uses vivid imagery to get our attention to make sure we really know how much God loves and how powerful His love is.

We don't see it because we aren't looking for it. But what if His love actually filled the area over the whole earth up to the atmosphere? Isn't God omnipresent? God is love; God is everywhere, so His love would be everywhere too. If the love of the Lord fills the earth, then we should be able to see His love everywhere around us. We can pray for other people to experience God's love, because He surrounds them too. It means that there's nowhere anyone can go that's outside of God's love. We just need to know how to recognize it.

Paul and David knew God intimately. They heard Him speak. They were corrected by Him and forgiven by Him. They *experienced* God. After long lives spent walking with God, they both were able to declare adamantly that God's love is everywhere, unlimited, perfect, and unconditional. Paul is speaking from personal experience when He states there is nothing that can separate us from God's love when we are in Christ.

You too must experience God's love for you. It's not enough to hear about another person's experience of it. You must hear God's voice, know His gentle correction and His gracious forgiveness. This is how we come to know His mighty love. You and I may not hear an audible voice like David or be taken up into the Third Heaven like Paul, but we can still have life-changing encounters with Jesus. It only requires that we be still, watch, and listen.

- Read the Romans passage twice slowly. What part of it stands out to you the most? Read it again asking God what He has for you in that section. What does He want to tell you about His love for you?

- What things have you believed could separate you from receiving God's love for you?

- Imagine yourself in the places you go regularly—home, work, church, kids' sports fields. Ask God to show you where He is with you in each place. Then, ask Him how He is showing you His love with His presence.

Encounter

Prayer

Beloved God, I confess that I can't fathom the depths of Your love, and my perception is messed up by the world's view of love. Help me to see and to understand that Your love is different and the only true love. Remove any barriers that keep me from receiving Your great love. Come to me that I may experience You, that I may know that I know that You are with me always, loving me forever. In Jesus's name, amen.

Covered

"This I declare about the Lord: He alone is my refuge, my place of safety; he is my God, and I trust him. For he will rescue you from every trap and protect you from deadly disease. He will cover you with his feathers. He will shelter you with his wings. His faithful promises are your armor and protection."
Ps. 91:2–4 NLT

"If you make the Lord your refuge, if you make the Most High your shelter, no evil will conquer you; no plague will come near your home. For he will order his angels to protect you wherever you go."
Ps. 91:9–11 NLT

"The Lord says, 'I will rescue those who love me. I will protect those who trust in my name. When they call on me, I will answer; I will be with them in trouble. I will rescue and honor them. I will reward them with a long life and give them my salvation.'"
Ps. 91:14–16 NLT

Encounter

IS THERE EVER A TIME IN LIFE that we don't need help, protection, or blessing? In Psalm 91, David makes a declaration and God responds with a promise. David declares in faith that God will be what he needs in his present circumstance. Then, God responds to David with a promise of blessing. God heard David and answered his prayer.

We are no different from David. God also hears us and will answer our prayers if we believe Him as David did. The problem is that we often don't believe and we don't wait for God. We are more likely to come up with our own solution as Abraham and Sarah did (Genesis 16), because it seems impossible that God will do it. Or maybe we believe God can do what we need, but we don't believe that He will do it for us.

It can feel like we are too small, too insignificant for God to rescue. It can feel like the "realities" of life are stronger and more real than God, so we give in to the "practical" ways of the world and stop waiting on God. We stop believing that He is who He says He is.

God will always be these things declared in Psalm 91 whether we believe it or not. He is always faithful even though we are not. He doesn't change with every trend and season the way we do. His character is always the same (Heb. 13:5), and He loves His creation always, no matter what (Mt. 23:37).

We each get to decide if we are going to believe God or not. It's not an easy journey, but He can make your life easier. It's not a straight path, but God does make your paths straight. The road is not comfortable or safe, but He will always be your safety and your refuge. It's an adventure to journey with the God of the universe.

Psalm 91 is an invitation to embark on a journey with the Most High God. Do you dare?

- Prayerfully read over the verses above. What from this list do you long to experience from God? Ask God if He's doing that thing for you. How can you see it? Is there anything you need to do?

- What does it mean to love God? It's okay if you don't know or you aren't sure. Remember that there is no condemnation. God understands our inability to love Him because He knows our capacity to receive love. Talk to Him about this. Ask Him how to love Him.

- Notice some of the blessings in the verses. Ask God to help you see how He is already providing some of these things for you. Take a moment to let that calm your fears and bolster your faith.

Prayer

Most High God, thank You for the blessings You provide to those who love You. Thank You for the constant protection You offer me that I don't even see. Please meet me in this place where I long for You to show up. Give me courage and grace to wait on You so I can see the goodness of the Lord in the land of the living. In Jesus's name, amen.

Waiting

"We live by faith, not by sight."
2 Cor. 5:7 NIV

"Abraham believed in the God who brings the dead back to life and who creates new things out of nothing."
Rom. 4:17b NLT

"GOD ALLOWS IN HIS WISDOM what He could prevent by His power." I mentioned earlier that this quote by Graham Cooke is hanging in my family room. It's so good and relevant to our faith journey that I'm referencing it again. It's a reminder to me to trust God when life isn't going the way I'd like it to.

There are so many things in life with God that don't make sense. As believers, we are called to live holding the tension of our current reality against the things we are believing from God. This is faith. Believing for what hasn't yet happened (Heb. 11:1). I love how Paul says it: "Abraham believed in the God who brings the dead back to life and who creates new things out of nothing." This is what we're doing when we choose to hold the tension of answered prayer and unmet need.

The faith journey includes seasons of waiting for God to act on our behalf. It's in that gap of waiting that we must hold onto faith. And yet, no matter how much faith we have, there will be moments when the waiting feels like too much. It's as though God knows our limits and likes to push us just past them. As long as we cling to faith in spite of our circumstances, God will grow us and He will eventually show up for us. I don't know why God works this way, but both the Bible and many personal testimonies show us that He does.

Noah worked over 100 years building the ark, not fully understanding why God told him to build it or where the water was going to come from. Abraham waited twenty-five years for the birth of Isaac and made some tremendous mistakes while waiting. Moses waited forty years in the wilderness before God called him back to Egypt. David was anointed as the next king of Israel and then had to wait over a decade before he actually became the king. Paul was in prison for four years waiting to be tried for crimes he didn't commit. Romans 8 says that creation is groaning as it *waits* to be freed from the curse of sin. The church is waiting for the return of the Messiah to set right the evil in the world.

What are you waiting for today? Physical healing, a child to come home, a new job, a spouse, a child to be conceived? None of us are exempt from waiting in this life. Waiting is hard. But God allows in His wisdom what He could prevent by His power.

Where does that leave us? How do we live in the tension?

We remember who God is and His heart for us. He has provided many times in the past. He is kind and patient. He loves us beyond measure. He is good and faithful, even when we are not. This allows us to trust Him. This allows us to believe who He is even when we don't see what we want to see. Knowing God's heart will allow you to see beyond your circumstances. Knowing God's love allows you to live by faith, not by sight.

I believe that waiting is God's greatest refining tool. Even the strongest believer will be challenged through waiting for God to do what He's promised. Although that's the point. This is how God grows us and heals us. God cares about our hearts more than anything else, because wholeness in our hearts and minds is what will make us free. So God allows in His wisdom what He could prevent by His power.

You can't endure the tension and waiting of life if you don't know God's love for you. Many people walk away from God when times get difficult. Jesus tells us this in the parable of the sower. If you know God's great heart and desire for you, then you will have the grace to wait for His good plans to be fulfilled.

He promises He is with you always; you're never alone. He promises that He will take care of you; you are held. So while you wait, while I wait, let's keep believing and trusting God's love for us.

- What are you waiting for? Tell God how it feels to wait so long. What doubts and fears rise up within you? Ask Him to speak to those feelings.

- Reread the Romans verse above. What does this tell you about God? Is this who you believe God to be for you?

- How well have you been waiting? Ask God if He sees you in the waiting. What is His response to your waiting? Ask Him to show you the grace He provides for you to keep waiting.

Encounter

Prayer

Oh God, my God. I feel that my life could be divided into seasons of waiting. There has been so much of it. Thank You that You've been present with me in all of it and that You always come through for me. Show me how to wait well, embrace the journey, and smell the roses as I hold the tension. Encourage my faith and heart as I wait. In Jesus's name, amen.

Provision

"You care for people and animals alike, O Lord.
How precious is your unfailing love, O God!
All humanity finds shelter in the shadow of your wings.
You feed them from the abundance of your own house,
letting them drink from your river of delights.
For you are the fountain of life, the light by which we see."
Ps. 36:6b–9 NLT

GOD IS INVESTED IN HIS CREATION, and He wants all of it to be cared for and to flourish. He loves His people and desires to care for them. He sustains all of nature: animals, vegetation, land.

This goes along with Jesus's reference to the lilies and birds in Matthew 6. God feeds the birds even though they don't harvest or store. He cares for the lilies even though they don't work. If nature matters to God, then how much more do we?

Encounter

We have an enemy who is seeking to distort our understanding of God. This enemy creates destruction and chaos and then blames God. We know this because the most popular argument against God is "Why is there so much evil in the world if God is real?"

The enemy wants us to see and to focus on the evil in the world. He tries to hide the good from us. Why? Because every good thing comes from God (Ja. 1:4). The news media is a perfect example. It's filled with negativity, fear-mongering, and destruction. The good news of God's faithfulness just doesn't get good ratings.

Satan wants us to miss God because we're so distracted by evil. You can see it even in the church. Many who claim to be followers of Jesus talk of the evil in the world and choose to doubt God rather than seeing the truth for what it is.

God's heart for all of creation is for it to be sustained abundantly—having more than what it needs to thrive. He wants to bless it with nourishment and shelter out of His own supply. And the whole world is His and everything in it (Ps. 24:1)! He owns the cattle on a thousand hills (Ps. 50). He says in Psalm 50:11–12, "I know every bird on the mountains, and all the animals of the field are mine. If I were hungry, I would not tell you, for all the world is mine and everything in it." He wants to provide for everyone on the earth, and He has the supplies to do it.

Care and provision are very personal. We all have very different, specific needs, and our God is a personal God. He wants us to see Him and know Him in His care for us. Every person gets to choose for himself to believe God and to receive from God or not. God doesn't force His care on anyone. In order to hear these stories, we must seek out personal accounts because they aren't going to be broadcast on the news.

I've talked to many people about their experience with the COVID-19 scare of 2020. I've heard from many believers that they felt held and cared for by God. My family, in particular, was able to pay off significant debt, go on our first family vacation in seven years, and buy a much-needed new family vehicle. Beyond material provision, we experienced great blessing in our family relationships, bursts of creativity, and overwhelming peace when the world was tearing itself apart.

I talked to one woman who shared something similar. She lost her job before COVID happened, but she saw it as a blessing because she was home with her kids when school was cancelled. She started her own business from home and it excelled. She and her husband were able to fulfill a long-time dream of buying a lake house. All during a global shutdown. This is what God does for His children.

God is offering you so much more than physical provision in this verse. He offers you spiritual insight, a new heavenly perspective, fullness of life, and emotional refuge and healing. He wants to give you everything you need!

We must start looking for God through this lens. Stop listening to evil and start pursuing Good. Get to know your Mighty God whose heart is for you and who wants to take care of you and meet you in your place of need.

- What part of the passage resonates most with you from the verses above? Journal the things it stirs within you. Ask God what He has for you in it.
- Ask God if there are ways that you're rejecting His care.
- How have you let the world's focus on evil shape your perception of God? Ask Him what is true. Ask Him to help you see all the good in your world.

Encounter

Prayer

Creator God, thank You that You take care of me. I know that it's because of You that there is any good in the world at all. Give me eyes to see Your goodness all around me. You are a good Father with a heart for all You've made. Show me Your heart. In Jesus's name, amen.

No More Shame

"So now there is no condemnation
for those who belong to Christ Jesus."
Rom. 8:1 NLT

"He has removed our sins as far from us
as the east is from the west."
Ps. 103:12 NLT

ONE MORNING I WAS AWAKENED by the sound of the garbage truck. My first thought was dread because we didn't take our trash can down to the curb. Our trash can was overflowing and it was two days before Christmas, which meant an unreasonable amount of trash would soon be added to it.

I was immediately filled with shame and condemnation. I thought, *How could I be so stupid? I should've known better or paid more attention.* I felt like a failure as an adult. I actually thought, *It's no wonder I'm not getting the things*

Encounter

I've been asking God for. All because I forgot to take out the trash.

I told my grandma. I thought she'd understand why I felt so foolish. But instead, in a comical voice she said, "I think you'll survive. If that's the worst of your troubles, then I guess you're doing okay." I was shocked! I expected to be shamed for my forgetfulness and irresponsibility. How could she be so nonchalant about my gross oversight? She almost seemed amused. It felt like a much greater offense to me. I felt so much shame and embarrassment. After all, the trash was in the driveway piling up, making us look like deadbeat slobs to the neighborhood.

This is condemnation. Any time you punish or shame yourself or feel like a terrible person because you think you've done something wrong, what you're experiencing is condemnation. My grandma didn't condemn me, and God wasn't condemning me either. (I've never seen anything in the Bible about forgetting the trash.) I was condemning myself. Although this example is absurd because it's just the trash, it's also perfect, because we do this often in life and need to be aware of it.

Any time someone responds in a way that's disproportionate to the circumstances, they've hit a landmine of lies. Clearly, there are some pretty deep lies I was believing. In fact, my response had nothing to do with the trash. Curt Thompson says that 80 percent of the conflict in marriages has nothing to do with the other spouse.[1] We are merely being triggered by our spouses and responding to beliefs we learned in childhood. This is true in any relationship. It's the closest relationships that trigger us the most, like being with your family for the holidays.

This verse says that God no longer condemns you. This doesn't mean that you won't *feel* condemnation. The enemy will condemn you as long as he roams the earth. He wants to keep you wrapped in your bondage. He wants to keep you away from the good God has for you.

When you condemn yourself, you do the enemy's work for him.

The good news is that we have a choice. Because God doesn't condemn us, we can choose not to condemn ourselves. The Bible says that God made us blameless and without fault. It says He doesn't remember our sins anymore (Is.43:25). If God doesn't remember our sins, then why do we? If God has made us righteous, then why do we condemn ourselves every time we make a mistake? That's no longer who we are. It's time to start believing what God says about us.

We can choose to see ourselves differently. We can choose to live in this new reality as children of God without stain or blemish. When we sin, we confess, receive God's grace, forgive ourselves, and move on like a toddler who falls but gets back up and keeps walking. You can decide to let it go, and God is encouraging you to let it go.

God loves you so much that He doesn't want you to carry this burden. Condemnation only hurts you, and Jesus died to carry it for you. He wants you to be free of it, because you are His child and He wants to make life better for you.

How do you let go? It's not easy. It takes awareness, practice, and patience, but it's better to move toward freedom than to continue in this bondage. First, recognize the triggers for what they are. Forgetting the trash was a trigger that had nothing to do with the trash. The triggers are a gift even though they feel so bad. Triggers expose the places where you are believing lies about yourself and about God. When you're paying attention to these, then you can combat them with Truth.

The yucky feelings won't go away right away. When you begin to recognize them, then you can stop living out of them and see your situation for what it is and what it isn't. You see the triggers and know they're there, but they no longer have the power they did before you noticed them.

I decided that this situation with the trash doesn't get to determine my reality or my identity. I'm good. I'm a responsible adult. God loves me and doesn't punish me for my shortcomings. Nor does He expect me to be perfect. Even dealing with a garage full of trash for the next week isn't a punishment unless I choose to see it that way. I can even be thankful for what was revealed by this silly scenario.

There is no condemnation for those who belong to Jesus. If He can forgive you, then you can forgive yourself. This applies to every sin you've ever committed and every sin you will ever commit. Live in the Truth, forgive yourself, and be free.

- Imagine your life without condemnation. How free would you be? Who would you become? What could you do? Ask God how to live in this freedom.

- Ask God what it means about His heart for you that there's no condemnation against you. Keep these truths close to mind so you have them to combat the lies the next time they come up.

- Start watching for triggers. Pay attention to the feelings within yourself as you go about your day. Notice irritation and feelings of offense. Ask yourself why you feel that way. Ask Him what lies you're believing about yourself and what is true about you.

Prayer

Father God, thank You that You hold nothing against me. Thank You that I'm free to forgive myself and live my life without condemnation. Please make me aware of the areas where I continue to condemn myself so I can give them to You and be free. Teach me Your truth so I can walk in it. I pray that the truth would burn away all of the lies within me. In Jesus's name, amen.

Identity

"Then God looked over all he had made, and he saw that it was very good!"
Gen. 1:31 NLT

"Now the serpent was more crafty than any of the wild animals the Lord God had made. He said to the woman, 'Did God really say, "You must not eat from any tree in the garden"?'

The woman said to the serpent, 'We may eat fruit from the trees in the garden, but God did say, "You must not eat fruit from the tree that is in the middle of the garden, and you must not touch it, or you will die."'

'You will not certainly die,' the serpent said to the woman. 'For God knows that when you eat from it your eyes will be opened, and you will be like God, knowing good and evil.'

Encounter

> When the woman saw that the fruit of the tree was good for food and pleasing to the eye, and also desirable for gaining wisdom, she took some and ate it. She also gave some to her husband, who was with her, and he ate it. Then the eyes of both of them were opened, and they realized they were naked; so they sewed fig leaves together and made coverings for themselves."
>
> Gen. 3:1–7 NLT

MY SEVEN-YEAR-OLD SON told me after church last week that there was a boy who called him a loser. I said, "You know that's not true, right? He doesn't get to determine who you are."

Consider how your parents raised you. God gave them the job. They're supposed to shape you, but you probably didn't stay in their mold.

We are shaped by our culture, our fear, and the lies we believe. We are shaped by criticism and correction from people around us. The reality is that if we don't pay attention, we are more likely to let ourselves be shaped by negativity than truth because negativity cuts deeper. It hurts and we don't like to hurt, so we correct ourselves so we don't have to feel that hurt again. Even if negativity stirs rebellion within us, it's still shaping us. We usually don't realize that we're letting all of those things determine who we are.

When I was in middle school, I had a favorite outfit that I wore every week. One day, a girl approached me and commented that she noticed I wore the same outfit a lot. I can't remember the exact words, but it had a negative connotation in my mind. I imagine that she had a snarky smirk on her face while she spewed judgement. Something like, "What's wrong with you that you wear that, like, all. The. Time?"

This person meant nothing to me, but her comment really bothered me, so I changed. I started writing down what I wore so I didn't

IDENTITY

repeat an outfit for nearly a month. I let another person I didn't like or trust shape my behavior and perception of myself. I let her determine who I was. I let it affect me so much that it's something I still remember so many years later.

The problem is that we're often unaware of the things that shape us. We have to start paying attention so we can be intentional about who or what we're letting shape our identity. We have to throw off the lies of the past and the lies of the present that threaten to define us and choose who we will become.

The reality is that as an adult, no one can change you. You have to agree to it and choose to change or not. You're not a victim. You get to decide. Will you receive identity from your Creator who loves you, other people who like you most of the time, or things that don't care about you at all—sin, fear, rebellion, or apathy?

God wants to be the one to shape your identity. He made you. He declared that you are good. He knows you better than anyone. He also knows how to give you good things better than anyone else. Jesus died to give you a special identity. This identity is something that you can only have access to when you are saved by Jesus's blood. (See Appendix A if you're not saved.) Once you are saved, this identity is a free gift for you just waiting for you to receive it. You must choose to claim it for yourself, to believe it, and to live it out.

God loves you more than any person on the planet. He's invested in your life and your future, not for His sake, but for your sake. He wants to see you succeed. He wants you to be free and happy. He knows what is necessary to make that happen. Look to God's heart for you. You can trust that the identity He wants to give you is perfect and will fit just right.

Encounter

- Read the Genesis 3 passage above a few times. Pay attention to the parts that stand out to you. What does the Holy Spirit want to show you about those things?
- Are you hiding from who God made you to be?
- Are you listening to voices that are holding you back?
- Ask God to show you who *He* says you are. Here are some verses to explore: Eph. 2:10; Is. 43:1; Gen. 1:3; Judges 6:11–12; Lk 3:22, 4:18–19; Eph. 1:4–8, 2:4–6, 2:19–22. Which ones resonate with you? Ask God what small steps you can take to start walking in your identity in Christ.
- Ask God to show you who or what from your past has shaped your identity. What lies have you been believing that are dictating your self-image and actions?

Prayer

Heavenly Father, I want to be the person You made me to be. I know that is the best version of myself and will result in the most fulfilling life for me. Help me to throw off the false identities that are holding me back. Show me who I am in Christ. In Jesus's name, amen.

Comfort

"All praise to God, the Father of our Lord Jesus Christ.
God is our merciful Father and the source of all comfort."
1 Cor. 1:3 NLT

"When doubts filled my mind, your comfort gave me
renewed hope and cheer."
Ps. 94:19 NLT

"Your promise revives me; it comforts me
in all my troubles."
Ps. 119:50 NLT

WHEN I THINK OF COMFORT, I think of kids with security blankets and stuffed animals sucking their thumbs. But I don't often see adults with these items. What do adults do for comfort? Where do you look for comfort? What do you do when your pain, physical or emotional, becomes too much? When you're hurting from rejection or fear? What do you turn to in order to make yourself feel better, or at least to lessen the ache?

Most people know that God doesn't always remove our pain. I'm tempted to say that the majority of the time He doesn't. He does speak life and truth into our pain so we can endure through it and even feel hope amidst it. *This is the power of God's comfort.* It's not temporary, but enduring. A perfect example of this is in Genesis 16:7–11. In it, God comforted Hagar. He didn't remove her pain. He told her to go back to her difficult situation and endure. The passage says that Hagar felt seen by God and heard in her distress, which is another way of saying that she felt comforted by God. She trusted God and was able to go back to her circumstances with peace and hope.

In Kings 19, Elijah was in need of comfort. In spite of all the victory he had seen with the prophets of Baal in chapter 18, he was afraid because Jezebel was trying to kill him. He believed that he was the only prophet of God left. God showed up for Elijah and spoke to him in a calm, gentle voice. God exposed the lies that Elijah was believing and told him what was true. Then, God gave Elijah instructions for what to do next. Elijah was able to follow the instructions to go back into danger because he had received comfort.

I imagine God speaking to Elijah like you would to calm a toddler. "Shh, shh… It's okay." You might pat their back to soothe them. Elijah calmed down, his mind quieted, his emotions settled, and then he was still enough to hear God speak to him. When he finally did, God told him what to do next and assured him that he wasn't alone, that there were other prophets who also survived. This didn't change the fact that Jezebel wanted to kill him, but it gave Elijah the comfort he needed to move forward with courage and peace.

COMFORT

This is an invitation for us. In whatever pain you face today, God wants to comfort you. After all, He is the "Source of all comfort." The invitation is to be still in His presence so you can hear the words of hope and assurance that He has for you. We can't hear God speak to us when we're wailing and lamenting our pain. It's important to express our feelings and emotions to Him, but then it's most important to be still and listen so that we can hear what He wants to say. This is how we receive His comfort, direction, and peace. He wants to speak to you just like He did to Elijah. Listen for His still, small voice. Wait for Him to speak.

God will show up for you because He loves you. He hates the pain you're in. He wants to equip you to walk the path before you and assure you that you're not alone. He wants to comfort you. He wants to give you the hope and peace that you need to move forward in the path He has laid out for you. The path may change, it may not, but if you take the time to be still with Him, you will find Him and He will show you the way (Jer. 29:13).

- Read 1 Kings 19:1–15, but imagine yourself in Elijah's position. What stands out to you? What does God want to show you about that?

- Read the passage again. Express your complaints and fears to God. See what He says in response to you.

- Slowly read the verses above. In what areas of your life and heart do you need to experience God's comfort today? Instead of asking Him to remove the thing that's causing the pain, ask Him what He is offering you to endure it and to be able to move forward.

Encounter

Prayer

God of all comfort, I need You now. Come near in this time of pain so I can see You. It feels impossible to live with it. I've begged you to change things, to remove them, or to provide. I don't often understand what You're doing, but I trust You. Give me the grace to surrender to You in this area. Give me the courage to see my circumstances through this lens that I have been resisting. Give me Your hope and assurance so I can move forward with courage in whatever You have planned for me. In Jesus's name, amen.

Fireproof

"When you walk through the fire, you will not be burned; the flames will not set you ablaze."
Is. 43:2b NIV

"Shadrach, Meshach, and Abednego replied, 'O Nebuchadnezzar, we do not need to defend ourselves before you. If we are thrown into the blazing furnace, the God whom we serve is able to save us. He will rescue us from your power, Your Majesty. But even if he doesn't, we want to make it clear to you, Your Majesty, that we will never serve your gods or worship the gold statue you have set up.'

"Nebuchadnezzar was so furious with Shadrach, Meshach, and Abednego that his face became distorted with rage. He commanded that the furnace be heated seven times hotter than usual. Then he ordered some of the strongest men of his army to bind Shadrach,

Meshach, and Abednego and throw them into the blazing furnace. So they tied them up and threw them into the furnace, fully dressed in their pants, turbans, robes, and other garments. And because the king, in his anger, had demanded such a hot fire in the furnace, the flames killed the soldiers as they threw the three men in. So Shadrach, Meshach, and Abednego, securely tied, fell into the roaring flames.

But suddenly, Nebuchadnezzar jumped up in amazement and exclaimed to his advisers, 'Didn't we tie up three men and throw them into the furnace?'

'Yes, Your Majesty, we certainly did,' they replied.

'Look!' Nebuchadnezzar shouted. 'I see four men, unbound, walking around in the fire unharmed! And the fourth looks like a god!'"

Dan. 3:16–25 NLT

We read in the Bible and have heard from well-meaning friends that God is "with us" in difficulty, but oftentimes it feels like an empty promise. I've often thought, *So what if You're with me if You aren't doing anything!* I'd like to suggest that God has great power and many gifts for us when we go through the fire if we're willing to receive them from Him.

You know the popular argument: If God is good, then bad things wouldn't happen. This argument is illogical because it ignores free will. Free will is the reality that each person who ever lived gets to choose to align themselves with God and His good ways, or align himself with Satan and his evil ways. We all get to choose.

Daniel, Shadrach, Meshach, and Abednego are a good example of this. We know that they were godly men who sought to honor their God in spite of the fact that they were exiles forced out of their homes into this foreign and defiled land. They didn't get hung up on "why" this was happening. They knew that they lived in a land of an evil king who was choosing evil. They chose to trust God's goodness regardless, and to focus on what they could do with what they had. They chose to defy the king in order to honor their God. God promises that He rewards those who seek Him (Heb. 11:6). Their reward was that they got to see God show up for them.

We all come to seasons throughout our faith journey when we don't understand what God is doing. We have times when we don't see Him working and we cry out, "Why!" Even Jesus cried out from the cross, "My God, my God, why have you abandoned me?" (Mt. 27:46). It's part of the faith journey. We don't understand suffering, so sometimes we get stuck on the "why" of the matter. Why is this happening? Why is God allowing this? Why am I sick? Why won't God fix this? You can probably add your own "why" question. The truth is there is rarely an answer. Sometimes we get to understand why after the trial, but rarely can we see it in the midst of our trials. This is the time that we must take God at His word, and trust that because He loves us so much, He will hold us and care for us.

Many times, we have to be willing to be thrown into the fire to see God differently and to be changed ourselves. Shadrach, Meshach, and Abednego would've never experienced God outside the fire in the same way they got to see Him in the fire. Some Bible scholars believe that it was actually Jesus who was with them in the fire. I like to think of it that

Encounter

way. I also think they were different after that experience with Jesus in the fire. The Bible doesn't tell us, but they had to be transformed. One doesn't go through something that powerful with their Savior without being dramatically changed by the experience.

The men were bound when they were thrown in, but they moved around unbound. The fire burned off their bondage. Have you ever heard a victory story in which a person had a decent, comfortable life and then decided to challenge themselves to make it greater? Me neither. People only change when their discomfort forces them to. I hate that we're this way, but we are. I am. I know that I don't move in a new direction unless I receive a powerful push of discomfort. God wants to remove your bondage—the lies you believe that are keeping you trapped. He loves you so much that He cares about your heart more than your circumstances. This fact has annoyed me over the years, but the freer I become because of His perseverance, the more thankful I am that He cares so much about my heart. I'm actually being changed, and you can be too.

- Read Daniel 3 asking the Holy Spirit to lead you in all truth:
    - In the first reading imagine the scene playing out. Feel it, smell it, imagine yourself in it.
    - Read it again and pay attention to what stands out to you. Where are you in the story? What do you feel as you endure this scenario?
    - Read it a third time and ask God what He wants to show you about how this relates to your life. What is God's response to you?
- Is there a fire that God is inviting you into? How do you see

it differently considering the gifts that God wants to give you through it that He can't give you any other way?
- What "why" questions are keeping you from seeing what God has for you? What might be a better question to ask?

Prayer

Dear Jesus, my Savior. This "fire" is so difficult and it scares me. Thank You for being with me in it. Give me eyes to see You and ears to hear Your voice. Give me grace to endure: to seek You, to trust You, and to keep waiting on You. I anticipate that You will show up for me and lead me to victory. In Jesus's name, amen.

Transformed

"But you are not like that, for you are a chosen people. You are royal priests, a holy nation, God's very own possession. As a result, you can show others the goodness of God, for he called you out of the darkness into his wonderful light."
1 Pt. 2:9 NLT

"For we are God's masterpiece. He has created us anew in Christ Jesus, so we can do the good things he planned for us long ago."
Eph. 2:10 NLT

"But now, [your name], listen to the Lord who created you. [Your name], the one who formed you says, "Do not be afraid, for I have ransomed you.
I have called you by name; you are mine."
Is. 43:10

Encounter

DON'T FORGET WHO YOU ARE.

When I forget who I am, I quickly slip back into old ways of thinking and acting that are based on lies and fear. I start living as though I was never transformed by God's power. I become consumed by feelings of scarcity and insecurity. Even though I know better in my mind, my heart can't shake the feeling that I'm not being taken care of because I'm not worth it. You likely have your own special place of torment you go to in your weakest moments. The human mind is very powerful. It can be your prison or your freedom.

Paul says to be transformed by the renewing of our minds (Rom. 12:2 NIV). We must know what is true and choose to cling to it even when we don't feel like it. There will always be moments when our circumstances don't match our beliefs, and it's in those moments that we must cling to what God tells us is true. It's important to hold the tension. Recognize the gap between where you are and what God has promised.

I often use this visual. It's a way to believe while also being honest about your circumstances. Imagine that you're holding the current reality in one hand, and the promise of God in the other hand. Hold them up to the Lord like you're showing it to Him. This is holding the tension. There's a gap between your hands, and you need God to fill it. Don't let go of the promise until He fills in the gap. Don't give into the lies, doubts, and fears. Cling to what you know is true against all odds. Choose to keep waiting on God. This is the only way for those subconscious beliefs, and ultimately your reality, to be changed.

God tells you who you are. You don't have to figure it out. Learn it and claim it. Walk in it with confidence. Write it down, keep it close, review it often. The Lord of Heaven's Armies is on your side, and He has chosen you, but only you can choose to receive His identity for yourself.

The world and the enemy will fight you. They want you to be defeated. They want you to be ineffective and unproductive in the Kingdom of God. Don't listen to the lies. Let them go and be who God has made you to be. God gives you all power by the Holy Spirit and the blood of Jesus to live freely as a beloved Child of God. Be who He says you are. You don't have to earn it; just receive it and live it.

- Read the Isaiah verse over a few times with your name in it. (It's okay that you insert your name. We aren't reading it for historical purposes, but as a promise from our God.) Each one of us is unique to God. He has special words just for you. What does God want to show you about who you are to Him?
- Of the verses above, which one resonates most within you? What does it mean to you? Ask God what He has for you in it.
- What small things can you do each day to resist the labels of the world and to start, or continue, walking in your identity in Christ?

Prayer

Father God, this has been an amazing journey! Thank You for showing up for me in all the ways that You have. Thank You for showing me more of Your great love for me. Teach me how to walk in my true identity in Christ. I want to see You and trust You every day. Keep these truths that I've learned close to my heart and mind as I continue to live in this fallen world. Give me eyes to see You all around me. Thank You that I am with You and You are with me amidst the evil and corruption in our world. You are still so good! In Jesus's name, amen.

Appendix A: Salvation

WHAT DOES IT MEAN TO BE "SAVED"?

John 5:24 says, "I tell you the truth, those who listen to my message and believe in God who sent me have eternal life. They will never be condemned for their sins, but they have already passed from death into life." Salvation in Jesus can sound very complicated, but it's not. There is a powerful supernatural exchange that takes place, but the Holy Spirit does all the work.

To be "saved" simply means that you have recognized your need for a Savior and asked Jesus to come into your life. It means that your name is written in the Lamb's Book of Life, and you will get to spend eternity in heaven with God and all other believers. It also means that there are unlimited resources of grace, blessing, power, and provision available to you while you're on the earth.

When you're saved, God adopts you as one of His own children, so you gain access to His life, power, and resources. It's as though you become part of a parallel universe. Although you're walking around in this physical space, you're also seated at the right hand of Christ in the heavenly realms (Eph. 2:6). I don't pretend to understand it all, but the more I believe it and seek to live it, the more I see evidence of it in my life. My father-in-law says it's all about favor. In Christ, we've been given abundant favor in all things, and we should be looking for it everywhere around us. I have noticed that when I look for it and start calling it out, then I see more. This is life in Christ.

There's a spiritual exchange that happens in that moment of salvation. First, you recognize that you need saving. That means recognizing that you're a sinner and that you can't be good enough on your own. This isn't about feeling bad about yourself. This is a freeing place to be because you can relieve yourself of the burden to try to be "good enough," whatever that means to you. With God, "good enough" means to make yourself holy. You can't do it. You don't even have the tools. The good news is that God doesn't expect you to. He wants you to let Him do it for you! *He* wants to make you "good enough."

After you've become aware of your sin, then you confess all of this awareness to Jesus and ask Him to come into your life and save you. Confession and belief are very important (Rom. 10:9). In exchange for your confession and sin, God gives you the Holy Spirit and His righteousness. You actually feel different in that moment of exchange. It's very powerful! You have to experience it to understand it. Otherwise, it just sounds crazy (1 Cor. 1:18)!

Salvation is a gift that God gives freely to those who ask Him. He wants you to have it so much that Jesus already paid the price for it whether you receive it or not. It comes by faith, so if you're struggling to believe it, ask God to help you. You must believe it to be able to receive it (Heb. 11:6). This is what it means that salvation is "by grace through faith." It's a gift freely given to those who believe and ask.

Once you are saved, your sins are removed from you as far as the

APPENDIX A: SALVATION

east is from the west (Ps. 103:12), and God will never see sin on you again. You are declared holy and blameless (Eph. 1:4) for all of your days: past, present, and future. Without that burden of sin, you are able to live your life in freedom. It can take time for our minds to catch up to the reality of what has taken place. That's why exercises like the ones in this book, or anything that keeps reminding us of what is true, are so important. So our heads, then our hearts, can catch up with our spiritual reality and we can live it out.

Here is a sample prayer for you if you're not sure what to say. There aren't any "right" words, but sometimes it helps to have a guide. Just tell God what's in your heart and He will meet you.

Salvation Prayer

Jesus, I see that I am a sinner. I've tried to figure life out myself and I can't do it. I need You. I believe that You died so I could be saved from my sins, live life to the fullest on earth, and share eternity with You in heaven. I lay my sin down at Your feet. I declare that You are the Son of God and that God raised You from the dead. I receive this gift You offer. Please come into my heart and be my Savior. Amen.

Here are some of the verses I referenced above so you don't have to look them up.

- Rom. 3:23: "We are all sinners and fall short of the glory of God."
- Rom. 6:23: "For the wages of sin is death, but the free gift of God is eternal life through Christ Jesus our Lord."

- Rom. 10:9: "If you confess with your mouth that Jesus is Lord and believe in your heart that God raised him from the dead, you will be saved."
- Eph. 2:6: "For he raised us from the dead along with Christ and seated us with him in the heavenly realms because we are united with Christ Jesus."
- 1 Cor. 1:18: "The message of the cross is foolish to those who are headed for destruction! But we who are being saved know it is the very power of God."

Acknowledgments

THERE ARE A NUMBER OF PEOPLE I want to thank who blessed me with support and encouragement throughout this writing process.

First, I want to thank my husband, Mike, for his continual support of me in the writing process. He created time, space, and resources that I needed to make it a reality. Along with editing the book, his constant love and affirmation showed me that he believed in me and my ability to finish this project.

I want to thank my bestie, Jennifer Davies. She's been my cheerleader and confidant since we were twelve years old! She was my first guinea pig and did the exercises so I could see if they "worked." She helped me tweak wording and ideas and assured me that God was speaking through them. She was often God's mouthpiece to me when I got discouraged, and she motivated me to stay the path.

Thanks to Mike and Marcy Gauch for years of loving encouragement. I am the person I am today in part because of their unconditional love and friendship. I have experienced God more fully because of their influence in my life!

I want to thank my dear friend Barb Smail for her love and encouragement. She tried out some of the exercises and gave me tips on capitalization. Her responses to our many talks helped me see that I might have knowledge worth sharing.

Thank you to all the ladies on the Zion Women's Retreat. You were the first to know of God's commission to me to write this book. Your follow-up inquiries were positive peer pressure to stay the path and get it finished.

To my publisher/editor, Emily Hitchcock, thank you for your diligent editing and all your efforts to get this book through production. It was a long, trying process, and I couldn't have done it without you.

Endnotes

WHY LOVE MATTERS
1. *Interstellar*
2. https://www.ministrysamples.org/excerpts/THE-SPIRIT-OF-GOD-BROODING-OVER-THE-DEEP-TO-PRODUCE-LIFE.HTML.
3. Benner, David. *Surrender to Love.* p. 23.
4. Tozer, A.W. *The Pursuit of God* (Camp Hill, Penn.: Christian Publications, 1982). p. 49.

TO KNOW AND BE KNOWN
5. Benner, Jeff A. Know, https://www.ancient-hebrew.org/definition/know.htm.

GETTING STARTED
1. Thompson, Curt M.D., *Anatomy of the Soul.* p. 67.
2. Brown, Sharon, *Sensible Shoes.*

Encounter

BELOVED
1. The idea of meditating on this verse was borrowed from *Anatomy of the Soul* by Curt Thompson.

PRESENCE
1. The Higher Pantheism

RESCUE
1. Of every place in the Bible that says God is "slow to anger" (nine times in NIV), eight of them are followed with "abounding in love" or "rich in love." The other one says "great in power." (Nah.1:3)

UNFAILING
1. New Living Translation.
2. Definition of "unfailing love" in my bible.

ENOUGH
1. Johnson, Bill. "Love Versus Fear." https://www.youtube.com/watch?v=CDc-4Vts1lU.

TRANSFORMED
1. This idea is suggested in the book *Sensible Shoes* by Sharon Garlough Brown. Pg. 149. The character, Katherine, explains the technique: "At the moment, we aren't looking at the text historically. We're reading it devotionally as prayer. As God's promise to you."

About the Author

LEANNE O'DONNELL is a published author, trained spiritual director, certified fitness instructor, and professional event coordinator. Leanne has experienced God and His great love for her through the roller coaster of life as a wife and mother.

Because of these experiences, her desire is to help others experience God in life-changing ways. Leanne's loves include her husband and their six kids, traveling together, exercise, and reading. She lives in Columbus, Ohio.

www.ingramcontent.com/pod-product-compliance
Lightning Source LLC
Chambersburg PA
CBHW022102090426
42743CB00008B/690